The Secret Behind Wisdom

* BLAISE K.TSHIBWABWA *

The Secret Behind Wisdom

The Secret Behind Wisdom

BLAISE TSHIBWABWA

The Secret Behind Wisdom

Malachi Publications

Toronto – Ottawa - Calgary

PUBLISHED By Malachi Publications

Conclusion, Bibliography and Content Copyright © 2015 by Blaise Tshibwabwa

All rights reserved under International Pan-American Copyright Conventions.

Published in Canada by Malachi Publications.

ISBN: 978-0-9917595-4-5

This is a work of fiction. Names, characters, businesses, places, events and incidents are either the products of the author's imagination or used in a fictitious manner.

Any resemblance to actual persons, living or dead, or actual events is purely coincidental.

We ask you to respect the author's imagination and work. Illegal reproduction in part or as a whole of this work is illegal.

Should you intend to reproduce this work or use parts of this work, please seek permission from the author.

Web: wisdomsecret.weebly.com

The Secret Behind Wisdom

The Secret Behind Wisdom

"For wisdom is a defense even as money is a defense, but the Excellency of knowledge is that wisdom shields and preserves the life of him who has it"

- Ecclesiastes

The Secret Behind Wisdom

To you Papa (Eli T. Tshibwabwa), this book I dedicate to thee. Your leadership excels the unexpected of the expected by most!

The Secret Behind Wisdom

Prologue

The Secret Behind Wisdom
Online at: wisdomsecret.weebly.com

The Secret Behind Wisdom

Prologue

All day, all the way, I push for the top gear_ so that like you one day, I may be a great Leader.

"To be or not to be" I can see and feel the touch of humility and the heavenly shield over thee_ and again the preacher says to be or not to be a leader; what is your legacy?

Despite your entire God given knowledge, you never take life on the edge.

Many are those who get to walk with you on a daily:

Yet again they say all of us who align in your family tree are lucky!

If having gravity was lucky, then why don't they understand that it's a BLESSING.

"The Lord is my shepherd..."
I constantly hear your voice echo in my heart.

To The Lord your entire you, you give and that includes your heart.

I salute and praise The Lord, because I know, He will never tear my heart apart.

"The Lord gave me something that no one else could give" And again your wise voice echoes in me.

A mentor like no other, your perceptions and approach towards life, an imprint I will keep forever.

A father that gives me power

A father who makes me feel like no other.

A father that I admire from near and afar.

A father like no other, and that's why I call you My Papa.

The Secret Behind Wisdom

The Secret Behind Wisdom

One

It was the morning before the next evening and the morning after the past evening. (Hahaha, that was just me making sure you were reading every word - OK let's do this again...)

"What are you doing this weekend?" Tiffany inquired of Lloyd, as he seemed overwhelmed with his day.

"Euh, I will be at cross iron mills to pick up a few things for my upcoming roadtrip to Daytona with my father" said Lloyd.

"Interesting! I wish I could have such an experience with either one of my parents" answered Tiffany.

"Oh dear, we've had a few trips together, but this one is more a man to man trip" Lloyd responded as he shook his head with an inexplicable smile on his face.

"Ok, you are waking my curiosity ... Spill some more, come on" Tiffany went on as she sat with her latte in front of him.

Nervous, Lloyd responded "how about, we finish this conversation after work, I walked to work today."

Tiffany smiled and accepted the offer with a head-shake as she walked away towards her cubicle.

Lloyd had been working in the niche of medical equipment sales for a few years and doing well for himself. The son of a well-established scholar, he passionately enjoyed reading classics and listening to echoes of the best-composed symphonies.

On the other hand, Tiffany, his business partner, came from a single parent household with no siblings and no contact to her extended family.

"Come on Lloyd, it is time to close business for the day and I want to hear your story" Tiffany said smiling as she was powering off her MacBook.

"Sure, let me just file this folder and we can call it a day" he responded to her as he closed the door leading to the records room.

The two friends closed their offices and began walking down 5th avenue. Unlike every other fall evening, the climate was still temperate allowing them to enjoy the promenade.

"We should stop by the Delta, they have a Starbucks their" Tiffany suggested as the delta was just a block away.

"Sounds like a fine plan, I can surely enjoy a hot chocolate and a banana cake at the moment." Lloyd responded with a smile as he took out a Starbucks gift card.

They entered Starbucks, waited in line and took their respective orders before they sat and commenced to devour each other's past experiences while growing up at home.

"No wonder, you can't wait to go on that road trip with your dad again!" Tiffany interrupted with excitement.

"That's right, the last long roadtrip we did together was back in the late 90s, so this is really one that I trust will remain engraved in our memories for many more decades." Lloyd acknowledged.

"I am sure you will enjoy every kilometer of that trip," Tiffany mentioned as she gave Lloyd a tap on the shoulder.

"It should, I don't see why not!" Lloyd answered back with a smile.

"By the way, Lloyd, do you realize, we've been in business for more than eight years and I featured three times in a row in the Young Leaders of Today magazine!"

"That's very true and I always meant to ask you, what do you mean when you reply to the interviewer for the article that you are a self made leader?" Lloyd asked as he took his shades off.

"Mr. Lloyd Okafor!" Tiffany responded with a smile "I consider myself a self-made and born to be a leader because of the way I was brought up. As we both know, I had neither siblings nor father to look up to; all I had was my mother and the great leaders of this world. I took what I needed and here I am today leading a powerful business with you!"

"Impressive Ms. Tiffany Labonté. However, I still think that there is a supernatural commanding force that is behind every leader out there including us." Lloyd responded.

"I don't disagree that at times, there is that push and determination that kicks in from I don't know where" Tiffany replied to Lloyd.

"That is what I am talking about, and I want to understand what it is," said Lloyd with a very affirmative tone.

"Tell you what?" Tiffany smiled; "when you succeed in your quest, come tell me, I will be patiently waiting for your findings!"

"Oh yeah, trust me, I will do up the puzzle dear" Lloyd said.

The two friends shook hands and went in separate ways.

The Secret Behind Wisdom

Two

A few days went by, and in the pursuit to fully and deeply understand the concepts of leadership, Lloyd invited Tiffany and his father Jacob Okafor for a brunch so they could both give him various insights on how they understood wisdom and where, was their source of leadership.

"Papa" said Lloyd "do you agree that a leader is required to be spontaneous?"

As he took a sip of his coffee, Jacob Okafor responded, "Yes son, a leader has to be spontaneous. To me, spontaneity is valuable and sometimes necessary."

"If I may add to that" interrupted Tiffany, "it is important to remember that the consequences would be disastrous if most of our life's direction were left to serendipity and happenstance."

"I fully agree on that and on another parallel, a leader needs to know how to plan because planning and evaluating performance with long-term goals and objectives in mind requires discipline, but this discipline inevitably leads to greater freedom." Jacob mentioned as he poured more juice in Tiffany's glass.

"Thank you sir," she acknowledged.

"Don't you worry about it Tiffany, and please do feel free to call me Jacob, I have been seating on the board of your company for the past five years" Jacob said as he began to chortle.

"Just give me a moment here guys, I am taking notes, I don't want to miss anything" Lloyd mentioned to his two guests as he continued to scribe in his pamphlet.

"Leadership also suggests movement!" Lloyd said as he stopped writing and looking at the other guests on the outdoor patio where they had been seated for the past hour. "_Tiffany, any insights on this?"

"Lloyd, did you go back to school and are using us to write a paper?" Tiffany responded in laughter with Jacob tagging along.

"I wish I could go back to business school with all the knowledge I have acquired" he responded with a sarcastic tone.

"Well, in that case" Tiffany said with enchantment, "I strongly think that leadership should suggest movement; because people need to know where they are headed. It is also a question that a responsible follower should ask the leader, and that leader better have an answer because no one will follow a person who does not know where they are en route to."

"I like that keep going" both Jacob and Lloyd said as they nodded with their heads.

"Yes, that's pretty much all I can think of on that, and also that planning is crucial for a leader. A leader has to be able to respond to and take advantage of changes."

"I agree with you on all grounds Tiffany. I am a person who was raised in the Christian faith, it is without question that God is the ultimate long-range planner.", Jacob said, "The purpose of God encompasses the whole range of eternity to eternity and extend itself to every part of his dominion."

"Dad", Lloyd interrupted, "Tiffany was not raised in the Christian faith, so when you give biblical fundamentals, don't be surprised if she wants more clarifications"

"Talk about a leader!" Tiffany jokingly said as she gave Lloyd a high five.

"Not a problem" responded Jacob and continued explaining his understanding, "From a short-range perspective, things may appear out of control, but God is always ordering all things in a specific way that they will reach a glorious result. In other words, plans are ordained by God"

"Impressive" Tiffany acknowledged.

"There is much more that I have to share, but it will be for next time as I have to rush out to a seminar" Jacob responded as he shook both hands of Tiffany and Lloyd and left the patio.

"I like your father, I was reading over the biographies of the board members and I was amazed to see that he has a Ph.D." Tiffany shared with Lloyd.

"Oh yes, he is a scholar of his own kind, I get the shivers myself when I look at his accomplishments because in all that he was very present in the family life" Lloyd responded.

"Can you give me a quick run down of what you know?" Tiffany asked intrigued.

"I can give you a run down, but it is long, I will tell you what I remember from the top of my head, but I have most of it written down at the office." Said Lloyd.

"I am all ears dear" Tiffany replied smiling and waiting to be astonished.

"Concerning his education" Lloyd mentioned, "he graduated from high school in 1967"

"Wow, I was not even born at that time" Tiffany said giggling.

"Same here" Lloyd responded and continued, "in 1970 he got his Bachelor of Science; In 1974 he got his MD, in 1978 he got his MMED, in 1986 he got the most sought after degree, meaning his Ph.D."

"Bam! And, that is the year I turned 7" said Tiffany as she continued eating her fruit salad; "Did he practice at all?"

"Oh yeah, he first started practicing in 1974 as soon as he got his MD he went all the way to 1998 when he decided to devote his time entirely to teaching and research"

"That is an incredible life he had, but why didn't you follow his footsteps?" Tiffany asked her peer.

"It is an outstanding career, I did try, but it did not work out as we both expected so I went the business direction instead" said Lloyd.

"I see, I see" Tiffany acknowledged; "you know the thing that gave me a sense of pride too, is when I see the professional organizations to which he is affiliated and then I saw our company too!"

"Yeah, he is in quite a few" Lloyd responded

"Yeah, the ones I remember from the top of my head are the Canadian Coalition on Global Health Research, The Radiological Society of North America, The Canadian Society for International Health and the Interagency Coalition on AIDS and Development"

"Wow, Tiffany, you got some memory!" Lloyd exclaimed himself and continued saying; "The thing that blew me away some years back, is when my brother told me that our father was on the Board of Governors for the Hamilton Future Fund"

"Wait a minute!" Tiffany said as she blinked her eyes a few times, "I read of that, and if I am not mistaken that is when they administered a fund of approximately $165 Million Canadian"

"Yeah, something like that _ so we are in good hands with him administering the funds of our little company" Lloyd said as he helped Tiffany stand from her chair.

"Thank you Lloyd_ I have to say that is some career I wish I could accomplish"

"You tell me dear! Oh well, as long as you lead well in your niche you should be good; remind me tomorrow if we have time, we shall look at his awards and publications" Lloyd said as they began to leave the coffee shop.

"You know, I'm up for it_ and in all those accomplishments, he continues to pray! That is impressive Lloyd, I am starting to understand a lot"

"A lot like what?" Lloyd asked cautiously.

"Nothing to worry about, but I am getting inspired by his accomplishments_ we shall catch up tomorrow" Tiffany responded as she hugged him goodbye.

The Secret Behind Wisdom

Three

"Oh my, I did not realize time was passing me by" Tiffany said as she entered the office "_ I bumped into your dad and we talked a bit and he gave me some interesting facts_ are you ready to take notes?"

"Shoot away, I am ready for the touch of wisdom," Lloyd answered as he took Tiffany's coat.

"First things first, we all agree that Organizations are good." Tiffany started.

"Yes, Tiffany, I do not see why they would not, but yes continue I am listening_"

"Good_ just making sure! So, Organizations are good and they gather multiple resources and focus them on a mutually desirable outcome. On the other hand, Well-led organizations can accomplish far more than any individual can hope to accomplish alone."

"That's the truth. But how many organizations are _but organized?" Lloyd asked.

"A number of successful business people are purposely keeping their operations very small--or working alone--because they feel that bigger is anything but better. In other words, that doesn't have to be the case." Tiffany continued.

"Interesting analogy, I really like that, please do carry on_" Lloyd replied as he took his notepad and pen.

"Good, because this is where it becomes a bit complex for me. I am going to say it as your father said it, but you will have to explain to me more clearly who is Moses

because all I knew about him was that he had the red sea opened_"
"Fair enough_ I will explain once you are done_" Lloyd agreed.

"Thank you_ your father explained to me that Moses was overwhelmed by the problems of leading a large number of people. His father-in-law invented what has become a thriving profession: Apparently, Jethro is history's first recorded management consultant.

He helped Moses to see that organization and structure are essential to effective operation. Not only is work accomplished more efficiently, but also people are better served and supported in doing the work."

"Interesting point, I never looked at it that way_" Lloyd acknowledged as he highlighted some of his notes.

"Thank you, but at least you know more about Moses_ so anyway, Moses discovered the importance of organizational structure when he was still a fledgling leader. The principle embodied here is that effective leaders create a structure that nurtures the health of those they lead.

Moses did this by handpicking potential leaders, training them and empowering them. Moses teaches that key leaders can still maintain some control--when problems arose, he still acted as a final arbiter. But through effective delegation a leader can multiply his or her effectiveness and better meet the needs of those who require personal attention."

"Tiffany, you should consider becoming a motivational speaker_"

"Ha, Ha, you mean I should be your dad's assistant for when he decides to be a motivational speaker"

"If you say so, I agree. So am I correct to say that you agree with me_ when I say that a strong leader is approachable and willing to allow others to tweak the structure of his or her organization, if doing so will strengthen it." Lloyd asked.

"Yes, totally, and in case you are not noticing that is exactly what we practice here Lloyd"

"Yep_ now to give you a run down on Moses, he is known to be the man who, was the friend of God. The story of his rescue from the water by Egypt's Pharaoh's daughter, of her adoption of him as her own son and his royal upbringing has charmed our hearts for decades until this day.

Moses has accomplished so much that I am sure if someone took the time to write on him, we would have several volumes thick like dictionaries. When talking about Moses you need to consider his virtues and vicissitudes of Moses the historian, orator, leader, statesman, legislator and patriot. His greatest honor, however, was the privilege of being known as "The Friend of God."

"I like what you are saying and I can see the passion in your eyes, keep on talking Lloyd_"

"Oh yes dear! It's giving me tears and goose bumps talking about such a great man_ Moses lived for 120 years, and the interesting thing is that we can divide them into specific periods, check this, the first one is *The first forty years*—from his birth until the flight into Midian. As Pharaoh's son, Moses learned how to be somebody.

The second forty years—from the flight into Midian to the Exodus. And there in desert places he learned how to become nobody.

The third forty years—from the Exodus to his own exodus. As the leader of God's hosts he learned that God was everybody—the One he could speak to face-to-face as a man speaks to his friends!"

"Wow, and can his remarkable life be viewed under more aspects?" Tiffany asked.

"Yes, we can view it in three other aspects_ the first one is the moment when he turned fully to God. The second one is the moment when he absolutely broke with the world. The refusal and choice of something must be carefully noted.

It is not enough to refuse—we must choose. We must back up a negative with a positive; and the third one is the moment when between himself and God there was the sprinkled blood, the blood of atonement."

"The blood of what?" Tiffany asked clueless

"The blood of atonement, I will explain later_ you also need to note that Moses is the Law-giver in Israel, supplies us with a fitting type of Christ. Taken together we have several similarities, which pastors and leaders can develop"

"By leaders, you mean Christians leaders I think_ and can you share any of those similarities because I don't remember Jesus opening a red sea_ all I know is that he walked on the waters of the sea and stuff_ Oh yeah he stopped a rain storm too."

"Impressive, Tiffany, you know more than I thought!"

"Whatever, I still went to church on Christmas and Easter and took religion in High School and university too!"

"Nice, I like, and to confirm, yes, they had a

similarity of both having control of the sea_ They were both preserved from the perils of infancy; both were tempted, but had mastery over evil; they both knew what it was to fast for forty days.

Solitude was their strength. Both fed a multitude. Another impressive thing was their face; they both had a radiant face. Both endured murmurings; like most they both were discredited at home."

"Lloyd, are you sure that you are not a preacher on evenings and weekends?"

"Hahaha_Tiffany, really_"

four

"Tomorrow is the big day! Are you all packed?" Tiffany asked Lloyd.

"Can't wait for the venture, picking up my dad from Toronto on Wednesday and we continue the road on Thursday together"

"I thought it was about 30 hours drive to Ontario_"

"It is yes. I'm doing a few stops along the way in Saskatchewan and Manitoba, see a few friends then continue to Ontario."

"Sounds like fun_ I will be here taking care of business and making sure that we stay on track so we can expand our company as projected."

"Thank you Tiffany, I appreciate this partnership_"

"Any time Lloyd, and you still haven't given me more insights on your dad's accomplishments_"

"Oh my, that's so true, tell you what, when I come back, we shall take time to go over that"

The morning came; the sun had not fully risen. The sky was of a remarkable color, blue with orange lines across it and glimpse of sun rays piercing through it. Lloyd took the wheel and off he was driving away on the TransCanada highway.

After several clockwise needle movements of his watch, Lloyd finally got to the doorstep of his parents' residence.

"Welcome my son; how was your trip?"

"It was well mum, long, but enjoyable, listened to a lot of music and took a lot of stops to rest."

"That's good, go freshen up, I'm almost done cooking, your dad should be here in a few minutes too."

"Ok_ I will be back"

The Victorian style home had not lost its touch of elegance; it was still on point just like when Lloyd and his siblings were still living at home.

"Hey papa, how are you?" Lloyd voiced as he hugged his dad.

"Hey_ Lloyd, I'm good. You must be tired I guess?"

"I am a bit, but I had taken a break so that helps quite a lot."

"Good, and are we taking the road tomorrow Hahaha?"

"Hahaha, papa, if you do the driving, then

yes! My bags are not fully opened"

"At my pace we shall reach destination in six months_"

"I think we can take the road in a day or two so that we enjoy the trip and maybe convince mum to come too"

And from the other side of the room, we could hear Lloyd's mum respond "Nope! If you want me to come, let's fly I can't seat for that many hours anymore after our Atlanta trip, I promised myself that any roadtrip over five hours will be done flying."

"Son, I will be in the reading room for a bit_"

"Papa, I actually meant to ask you something; I wanted to know_ how does one lead with determination, wisdom and respect; I want to understand and grasp that_"

"Are you still on that, we spoke of that when I was out west?"

"Yes papa, but I feel like I need more" Lloyd responded.

"I hear you, grab a Bible"

"A bible and a notepad or_"

"It's up to you son, but grab a bible and your attention_ so turn to your bible in Joshua 1: 1-9 ... And read"

"After the death of Moses the servant of the Lord, the Lord said to Joshua son of Nun, Moses' aide: "Moses my servant is dead. Now then, you and all these people, get ready to cross the Jordan River into the land I am about to give to them—to the Israelites.

I will give you every place where you set your foot, as I promised Moses. Your territory will extend from the desert to Lebanon, and from the great river, the Euphrates—all the Hittite country—to the Mediterranean Sea in the west. No one will be able to stand against you all the days of your life. As I was with Moses, so I will be with you; I will never leave you nor forsake you.

Be strong and courageous, because you will lead these people to inherit the land I swore to their ancestors to give them. "Be strong and very courageous. Be careful to obey all the law my servant Moses gave you; do not turn from it to the right or to the left, that you may be successful wherever you go. Keep this Book of the Law always on your lips; meditate on it day and night, so that you may be careful to do everything written in it. Then you will be prosperous and successful. Have I not commanded you? Be strong and courageous. Do not be afraid; do not be discouraged, for the Lord your God will be with you wherever you go."

"Amen" the two responded when Lloyd finished reading.

"This is where the principle of courage and risk-taking for a leader kicks in my son_ Leaders need courage to make the tough decisions they're faced with every day; and as you can see, Joshua certainly faced such a crisis in his leadership role. Not only did he have to contend with the military powers rooted in the Promised Land, but he also had to face them with an untrained band of nomadic shepherds."

"_But Papa, where do these great men get

so much courage?"

"In this case Lloyd, God realized Joshua's need for courage and gave him guidance that would strengthen his faith. First, he reminded Joshua of his faithfulness to keep all of his promises as it states in verses 3 to 6. God had pledged to give the land to his people and he would fulfill that pledge. Joshua's success didn't rest on a military strategy or well-trained army, but on the faithfulness of God. Second, God commanded Joshua to meditate on his words that Moses recorded in the five books of the Pentateuch highlighted in verses 7 to 8.

The "Book of the Law" would give the wisdom and encouragement Joshua would need to courageously lead the nation. Third, God promised to be personally present with Joshua as you read in verse 9. No matter how intimidating the enemy or how rebellious the people; Joshua would not have to face them alone. God would always be at his side."

"That's quite something Papa but_"

"_Before you say more son, you need to understand and believe that the same sources of courage that empowered Joshua are available today for any leader who will accept them. When faced with a risky business decision, the godly leader will look to God in prayer and to God's revealed Word for the perspective, wisdom and courage needed to make the right choice_ if I may ask you, what situation are you now facing that requires courageous leadership and risk-taking?"

"My dear Papa, if I start, we shall be here for a while_"

"Well, let God's words to Joshua supply you with the courage you need son."

"Amen; I have always wondered if there is

any such thing as "a sure thing"?"

"Son, in this world nothing appears to be certain; many of us come to discover that our sense of being in control is only an illusion-we cannot control the outcome of even a single day. There is only One who exercises sovereign control. Read Hebrews 6:13-20 in your own time, to look at the only real anchor for the soul."

"Thank you Papa, the 9th verse in Joshua 1, has really touched me, you see where it says: Haven't I commanded you? Be strong and courageous. Do not be terrified; do not be discouraged, for the LORD your God will be with you wherever you go."

"Yes, it is a powerful scripture. I want you to take a mental note of this, leadership, by its very nature, inspires people to move in directions they would not otherwise have been willing to take. From time to time, good leadership requires excursions into unexplored territory, and draws on a leader's courage. Lack of courage demonstrates the high cost of failure."

"Hmm, I like that, that's deep_"

"As a good leader son, you "fix what's broken." Great leaders "fix what (to others) isn't broken." Ezekiel confronted a highly successful king and told him his life, though successful, was immoral and needed fixing. Though his life was on the line, Ezekiel had courage to risk everything."

"I see, so when Jesus cleared the temple, can we also say that he gave a powerful example of both courage and risk-taking that came from the wellspring of deep conviction."

"You are right my son, and I can see that you understand the principle of courage and risk taking."

The Secret Behind Wisdom

"That is because I am being coached by the best mentor_ you papa"

"Thank you son that is very humbling_ another important factor that ties onto leadership is to be a learning organization_ I am taking the example of an organization since you run your own business_"

"Yes, I am listening and taking notes papa"

"As we all know, following a smashing success, it's easy to kick back and rest, to assume that current knowledge and achievements will assure future success."

"Very true, I think Tiffany and I have done that in the past_"

"Yes, I remember those board meetings Lloyd, well as you know now, that's a dangerous attitude. When nations, organizations or teams stop learning, they're setting themselves up for failure."

"I surely don't miss those days papa"

The Secret Behind Wisdom

"I don't blame you son_ and as you may have heard and seen, *those who don't learn from history are destined to repeat it*. Effective leaders know this. They do their best to create an atmosphere that encourages learning within their organizations and teams. They remember the principles gleaned through past experiences, and they help their people to apply them to new situations."

"Wow, Papa, you just gave me a good punch there_ Hahaha"

"Hahaha, son, there is more to come_ right these two questions down and answer them truthfully_ what are you currently doing to open yourself up to new ideas?"

"Ok_ next one"

"The next question is what structures does your present organization have in place to stimulate learning?"

The Secret Behind Wisdom

"I like that one because we just revised that last few weeks_"

"Good, look at it this way son, we do not teach advanced engineering mathematics to first graders. A lengthy process of development and learning is necessary before people are ready to tackle these more sophisticated subjects. In a similar way, God gives us greater amounts of illumination as we respond to the light we have already received."

"That's true, hence the reason why continuous improvement requires continuous learning. Meaning that only the learning organization will, over the long haul, continue to grow."

"I agree son, what time is it by the way?"

"It's 11pm_are we good to continue or you want to continue tomorrow?"

"I'm good to share my wisdom, are you still ready to receive?"

"Yes I am!"

The Secret Behind Wisdom

The Secret Behind Wisdom

five

"Papa, before you go any further_ I meant to tell you that I really appreciate you and love you. I am proud to have you as my father."

"Thank you Lloyd, I am proud to have you as my son and friend."

The two hugged and decided to end their intense conversation for the night and each went to their respective rooms.

As Lloyd entered his room, he closed the door behind him and went on to his window. His mind, travelled back into time from when he was a toddler. Happy days and rainy days, papa and him playing, doing homework together and driving around town together.

As Lloyd sat by his bedside, he reminisced on a heart touching conversation they once had during a family evening conversation.

Papa had sat all the kids down in the family room and told them he had some important things to tell them that day. He wanted to speak of their future.

Lloyd sat there and the talk papa had given that evening all came back to him word by word…

"There comes a time in the life of every girl and boy when she and he must change from childhood to womanhood and manhood; a person cannot always remain a child. Until this time arrives, the person is very dependent and must lean entirely upon their parents' advice; but as their mind begins to mature, they should be taught the necessity of weighing matters well and of finding out God's will.

The Secret Behind Wisdom

Until the present time all you have done has been at the suggestion of us your parents, but it will be different in the future. With the teaching we gave you, you are able to look to God for your direction.

I want you to take things to the Lord in prayer and become satisfied within your heart that my advice is according to the Word of God.

You must not think you haven't needed the teaching and the guidance you've had this far in life; and you will need more careful training than you've ever had. The point I want to impress upon your mind is that there's an element within you, called self that you must learn to control.

There are many other things my children that I want to talk to you about soon, but you must be patient a little longer. In the meantime, however, you may ask me any question you please, and I'll answer you.

The Secret Behind Wisdom

Don't go to other girls or boys with these things, but come to us. We shall always be glad to explain to you anything that seems strange.

When you're old enough to desire the knowledge and to form the questions, you're old enough to receive an answer to your questions. Come to me often: what seems strange to both of us we can take to God in prayer, and let him teach us.

Another thing you must do is to turn away from bad associates. Avoid girls or boys who say, 'I'll tell you something if you will promise not to tell your mother or father.'

Remember that anything you could not tell either one of us would not be worth hearing; for it's sure to be something unclean or vulgar. Conversing with such people won't help you draw close to the Lord nor to know His will concerning you.

Much less would it help you to meditate upon the pure and holy things of God?

To elevate your soul, my children, you must become serious, and seek only those companions whose conversation is kind, gentle, and modest. I believe your desire is to become more like Jesus and to prepare for heaven.

So, meditate upon God, and you will grow in the grace and knowledge of Christ. Misspent moments are so much of life and character thrown away; be careful to use them all in God's service.

This being said, us too your parents will make an effort and a commitment to consult with our children with various issues, every day conversations and we shall come to you to seek also advise."

Lloyd thereafter fell asleep with those cherished memories.

Six

"Good morning, would Tiffany be available please?"

"Yes, may I ask who is calling please?"

"It's Reverend George returning her call."

"Thank you, would you mind holding the line?"

"Certainly, go ahead."

The administrative assistant left the front desk promptly and followed Tiffany in the office kitchen area.

"Hey Tiffany, I got a Reverend George on the line for you_"

"Oh my! Chantel, transfer him to my phone, thank you so much_"

"Allo, Reverend George, I have Tiffany on the line, you may go ahead."

"Thank you, young lady"

"Allo Reverend George, thank you for returning my call, how are you?"

"I am well Tiffany, and how are you and your mum doing?"

"We are well thank you."

"_Good to ear, so I am listening how can I be of help?"

"Well, things have been kind of better now between the two of us so I wanted to thank you for the support you gave us."

"Not to worry my child. Everyone needs a life do-over. Just like the kids on a playground, the concept of a "do-over" is well known. When they're playing basketball and the ball sticks between the backboard and the rim, a chorus of "do over" spontaneously erupts. It's an unspoken rule that every kid knows_ sometimes as adults we wish we could resurrect the rule in our own lives.

When we miss a bill payment, we long to be able to appeal to the utility company for a "do-over." When we speak a thoughtless word that hurts another person, we wish for the same."

"That is true, so how can we make the reality of the "do-over" active in our life once again?"

"Truth be told, this concept usually doesn't work in our adult lives and relationships without a good deal of work and humility on our part. We bear the consequences of our mistakes until regret grows and we thereafter ask for forgiveness.

The Secret Behind Wisdom

That's when grace can intervene, and the person we've harmed can forgive. Many of us find confession especially difficult because it cuts at our dignity and self-worth. When we confess we admit our mistakes and failures. We assume that these admissions don't make us look very good. When we're "man enough" to confess our wrongs, God can choose to pour out his blessings for the next phase of our lives."

"Thank you Reverend George, I appreciate these words."

"You are welcome"

"I will and thank you again."

(Meanwhile on the other side of the country…)

"Good morning Papa, Good morning maman"

"Morning Lloyd" the two responded at the same time as they all sat at the breakfast table.

"Did you all sleep well?"

"Yes we did, did you?"

"Yes I slept well, by the way, papa you speak Latin, and I meant to ask you what does Carpe diem mean?"

"It means, "Seize the day," and it certainly echoes a valid objective. We do need to seize each day because we don't know whether tomorrow will come or just how much of this life remains for us.

Despite all of our advances in safety measures, in industry and transportation, and all of our progress in the medical field, life still maintains a measure of unpredictability for us today.

Accidents still happen, and people still suffer from strokes and coronary artery disease, often seemingly out of the blue. Nearly everyone has a story to tell regarding a friend, family member or coworker who has experienced something like this."

"Interesting point Papa, so when was the last time you volunteered to do something in service to another person?"

"As a father, I have done several selfless things to serve you my children and as a husband, I have helped and served my wife numerous times without her asking."

"Hahaha, you got me good their papa"

"Hahaha, son, it is what it is! _ That is the paradox of serving. When we give ourselves away in service, we find ourselves. When we empty ourselves in service, we find fulfillment. A lot of people search for identity and self-fulfillment.

The Secret Behind Wisdom

Most look for it in repeated highs of promotions, exotic vacation or an endless parade of worldly possessions. But real fulfillment comes from serving God by serving others. When we give ourselves away in service to others, we find meaning and joy in life that selfishness can never equal."

"Nice, that is deep, I like that analogy."

"Guys eat, I don't want left over breakfast_" Lloyds mum interrupted.

"Yes mum, no left overs today. We will not have leftovers or a Y2K worry_ Hahaha"

"Oh my God! Do you remember all the buzz they had put around that Jacob?"

"I do remember that honey, and it's funny because I was reading this article at the airport the other day, and it was saying how

Ironically, most of us have zero understanding of computer code.

The apostle Paul said that wisdom is much the same way. Unless we have the Holy Spirit to help us know the language of God's wisdom, we won't really understand it.

"The person without the Spirit does not accept the things that come from the Spirit of God but considers them foolishness, and cannot understand them because they are discerned only through the Spirit" People who don't have the Holy Spirit dwelling within them quite naturally struggle to grasp spiritual wisdom—God's Word, his desires, his character, his values.

It also mentioned that God's wisdom often seems foolish to non-Christians. It's like a foreign language to them. But when people trust in Christ as Savior, God sends the Holy Spirit to dwell within them

They can begin learning God's wisdom while the Holy Spirit helps them understand it. In the Bible God speaks the language that drives us—our spiritual operating system. If we want to know God's wisdom so that we can process the joys and trials of everyday living, we need to turn often to God's Word and ask the Spirit to help us understand it."

"Eloquent I must say_ so papa will it be wise to say that_ Actually let's imagine a marriage in which the husband dutifully earns a living to pay his family's bills, takes care of the house and cars and sees that his family has the clothing and other things they need. Yet, he has lost all his tenderness and passion for his wife."

"My son" Lloyds mum interrupted "that is without question a non healthy marital relationship!"

"I agree mum, and can also be called Productivity without passion. Just as the partners in a marriage can lose their passion for one another and yet carry on, a similar situation can occur in relationships between believers and God. It's like at times when I compare my current relationship with Christ to what it was like when I first began following Him, at times I am not as passionate about knowing Him, being with Him and worshiping Him as I was back then.

Just like at times I find myself busy serving Him without bothering to further cultivate my relationship with Him?"

"Son, Sadly, like a marriage without passion, our relationship with God can go through a period during which spiritual passion wanes. We serve the Lord more out of habit or duty than out of a desire to know God more deeply.

Consider this possibility: God might occasionally want us to stop doing for Him so that we can concentrate on being with Him and recovering the love we had at first. Many dry marriages have been renewed.

Dry relationships with the Lord can experience renewed passion and vigor as well. Put your relationship with Christ first, then let your service for Him follow as a natural response." Jacob answered his son as he poured more tea to everyone.

"Well, in regard to that, as your mum, what I can say is that in our spiritual journey, praise and thanksgiving are like a yellow line, keeping our hearts on track. But it doesn't take much to veer off course, does it?

_ we've all heard of the doctor who is in terrible physical condition or the plumber whose house has leaky pipes. When you do something for a living, as these people do, it's sometimes hard to stay motivated to keep your own life in order. Praise and thanks to the Lord are key ingredients in a healthy relationship with God.

We need them as much as we need fresh air. Praise isn't just an outward gesture; it reveals what's inside us—the attitude we have toward God.

When we offer meaningful thanks, we acknowledge that God's goodness deserves our recognition and awe. Every gift comes from his hand. Nothing we've done grants us the sun's bright rising or peaceful slumber at night—it all comes from God's good hand.

Remember this, God doesn't demand that we follow certain daily requirements. Maybe that makes the routine more difficult. We are responsible for taking the time to bow before him and offer our praise and thanks.

The Secret Behind Wisdom

When we skip this routine, we become like those drivers who disregard the center line—a potential accident waiting to happen. But when we take the time to regularly focus on and praise the God who loves us, he helps us stay on track."

"Thank you mum, I appreciate these words of wisdom, just a quick question though, are you sure, you and dad were not missionaries somewhere? Ha, Ha, Ha"

"Yes, we've been missionaries in our home trying to keep up with you and your siblings!"

The Secret Behind Wisdom

Seven

"Well, I can attest that you have been very successful at that my dear parents."

"Thank you; and my son, remember that the ability to master our mouths, watch our words and tame our tongues demonstrates a level of spiritual and emotional maturity. The opposite is true as well. An inability to control our speech shows immaturity, and it can inflict great harm on our relationships.

Solomon addresses the importance of controlling our words by contrasting positive and negative speech. In each case, the effects end up as opposites: peacefulness or wrath, knowledge or folly, healing or a crushed spirit. In other words, when we fail to control our tongue, we don't just fail to give, or be, a blessing. We also cause a wound that can rupture a relationship.

The approach you can use to tell if your tongue is under control is that you won't say anything about an individual that you can't say directly to that person. You resist the urge to exaggerate. You consciously examine your thoughts and remove gossip and rumors from your conversations. You keep in confidence a personal matter that someone else shares with you. Further, you learn to speak positive words. Appropriate words communicate affirmation, comfort and healing."

"Thank you maman. That reminds me of proverbs 15 actually, _ you know how it says that a soft answer turns away wrath…"

"Yes, very true."

"And as I have always told you my son, the tongue is a two-edged instrument of power.

The Secret Behind Wisdom

With it we can lash apart a loved one, leaving deep scars. We've seen our child's confidence fade after our tongue strikes a blow. We've grimaced after thoughtlessly slicing our husband apart with our words. The tongue has an unequaled power to destroy.

But it also has the power to build up and to heal. We can wield it to build a mole-sized self-image into one that is majestically confident. We can use it to offer solace for the open wounds of those around us.

For example saying: "You look great!"

"Good for you!"

"I love you."

"I forgive you." — Can transform human life.

The Secret Behind Wisdom

It has the power to destroy. It has the power to heal."

"Yes, it is something we remind our new employees during orientation."

"Oh wow, they must be wondering what type of company they got themselves into_ don't they?"

"They seem a bit on the chock side at the beginning, but as the orientation progresses, they participate more and as a result we have a very healthy workplace_ it reminds me of a lot, more especially the day I left home_"

"Oh, I remember that night too son, it was hard for your mum and me to see you go, but we prayed for you that where you went, you'd not forget the teachings we gave you."

"Thanks papa, well, it was not easy. I still remember how the two of us spoke in front of your room door and you gave me $60.00 to help with my gas or first groceries_"

"Yes, I remember that very well too. It was a big adjustment after you left, but I thank God that today you are settled and aiming at higher grounds."

"_Talk about adjustment, I was not pampered to the warm meals anymore, but that period was very crucial in my life and I am glad, you and mum somehow encouraged me during my ups and down. Can you believe that I ended up in Sudbury seeking the real me?"

"Did you just say Sudbury?" the two parents repeated as they looked at each other.

"Sudbury yes. I ended up there for six months and if you recall that is when you were sending the most heart warming emails of encouragement.

The many emails I received from you at that moment in life really crafted me and are engraved until this day. So, I want to thank you both for that."

"You are welcome son and may the blessing of the most high continue to bless you as you evolve in life_ for every challenge in life, we all need support. It's hard to do it alone, and praying is no different"

"Thank you_ I must say that period of my life was something_ when I look back, I can see somehow that what helped me make it through is all the teachings given here at home, the thoughtful emails."

"You know Lloyd, when the proverbs say the fear of the Lord is the beginning of knowledge, it's a serious and deep statement that we often overlook, yet to know wisdom and instruction make it that a wise man will hear and increase in learning, and the person of understanding will acquire skill and attain to sound counsel so that he may be able to steer his course rightly_"

"_Hence the reason we also say the Lord gives skillful and godly wisdom; from his mouth come knowledge and understanding" Lloyd's mum added.

"Son, you see, it's not magic or rocket science on how to become a trustworthy and humble leader in your household, business and ventures. When you understand righteousness, justice, and fair dealing in every area and relation; you eventually understand every good path.

Skillful and godly wisdom enter into your heart, and knowledge becomes pleasant to you. Discretion watches over you and understanding keeps you clean and safe from perverse things, people with crooked ways. _ you are laughing_"

The Secret Behind Wisdom

Eight

Jacob smiled as he continued to speak to his son,

"Wisdom will eventually translates itself even when you decide to have a serious relationship with a woman. You will not get caught up with one that has a storage of flattering words. One who, is ready to ruin her husband.

Picture this son, you and I both know that as a man, it is important to have a respectable woman by our side. It is easy to get carried away because some women have lips that drip honey as a honeycomb and have mouths smoother than oil; but in the end, you realize that she is bitter as wormwood, and as sharp as a two-edged and devouring sword.

I will let your mum talk more to that in a few but to come back to our conversation, a major secret and powerful asset is that you need to lean on, trust in, and be confident in the Lord with all your heart and mind and make sure you do not rely on your own insights or understanding.

In everything you do, recognize, and acknowledge Him, and in return He will direct and make your paths straight and plain.

As humans, when we get the big positions at work, the evolving business, money and stuff we get distracted and it gets to our heads. However, my son don't be wise in your own eyes; reverently fear and worship the Lord and turn entirely away form evil because in doing this, it will be health to your nerves and stamina, and essence and moistening to your bones."

Lloyd was positively nodding his head as he heard the words his father was sharing with him.

"_Keep and guard your heart with all vigilance and above all that you guard, for out of it flows the spring of life. It is very vital that as a leader you put away false and dishonest speeches, and willful and contrary talks.

Instead, you should let your eyes look right on with fixed purpose, and let your gaze be straight before you. Wisdom my son, is like a woman.

Prize wisdom highly and exalt her, and she will exalt and promote you; she will bring you to honor when you embrace her.

Wisdom gives to your head a wreath of gracefulness; a crown of beauty and glory. It all locks in together. As you go up through the ranks, and your ventures

The Secret Behind Wisdom

expand, please son, remember this and pass it on to your children too. Do not portray a proud look, never overestimate yourself and underestimate others.

Refrain from lying and from causing heartbreaks and hurting people's feelings. Do not have a heart that is keen in manufacturing wicked thoughts and plans, nor become a false witness who breathes out lies no matter what the cost is. That is because hatred stirs up conflicts, but love covers all wrongdoings.

As a leader, your words have to be a source of righteous feed and guide many. As your father, I am not really into sports and I am glad to some extent because for a fool, it is a sport in itself for him to continue and plan his wickedness whereas to have skillful and godly wisdom is a pleasure and relaxation to a man of understanding! Look at us!" Jacob said as he stood to grab an apple.

"Ha, Ha, Ha nice analogy their papa. But yeah, I totally agree, I am getting wisdom and I am very relaxed."

"Yeah and another thing to keep in mind is that a wicked person will always end up in an awkward situation where destruction strikes them, but most of the time if not always, the desire of an honorable man is always granted to him. Swelling and pride never come alone, they always have emptiness and shame that tag along for the ride."

The Secret Behind Wisdom

Nine

The conversation between Jacob and Lloyd became intense and profound that the two were having second thoughts about their road-trip.

"Another thing you have to realize Lloyd is that riches is not everything in life. Some people consider themselves rich, yet they have nothing to keep permanently; others consider themselves poor yet they have great and permanent riches.

When you are rich, you can almost buy anything. As we say, money talks. This is now to the point where you can buy your way out of a threatened death just by paying a ransom, but when you look at the so-called poor man, he does not even have to listen to threats from those who envy him.

Build your empire little by little because it will increase its riches and will last for decades instead of doing every single crooked thing to grow your business. When you earn wealth in haste or unjustly, it will dwindle away.

As your father, it is my responsibility to leave you, your siblings and your children an inheritance of moral stability and goodness. When it comes to riches, I am not worried because the wealth of the ruffians will find its way eventually into your hands.

As you become more and more wise, you will suspect danger and cautiously avoid debauchery, but a fool bears himself insolently and is arrogantly confident.

I have continuously repeated to you that you need to work hard. This is because in all labor there is a profit, but idle talk leads only to poverty. When you work hard for your success and advancement, you end up with a calm and undisturbed mind and heart.

It becomes the life and health of the body, but envy, jealousy, and anger are like rottenness of the bones.

As a leader_ I keep referring to you as a leader my son because everyone is his own leader. We encounter challenges and all sorts of frustrations, but a principle to stand on is that a soft answer turns away anger. It's no need to use heinous words because they only stir up anger.

When one is wise, his tongue voices out knowledge rightly, but the mouth of the self-confident fool only pours out idiocy.

Humility comes before honor. This is the best slogan you can ever have for your own-well-being! I am thankful to God that you and your siblings turned out the way you did because a wise son makes a glad father, while a foolish one despises his mother and puts her to shame.

Even as the main guy in your business, never refuse nor ignore instruction and correction because in refusing that you only despise yourself.

Instead follow reproof and get understanding. By listening to reproof that leads or gives life, you will remain wise.

The reasoning behind this is simply that pride goes before self-destruction, and an arrogant spirit before a fall. It is far better to be of a humble spirit with the meek and poor than to divide the spoil with those who are proud.

If you deal wisely and observe God's word and counsel you will find good, and when you lean on and trust in, and put all your confidence in the Lord Jesus – you will be happy, blessed, and fortunate.

When you are wise in heart, people from your entourage and people around you will call you prudent, understanding, and knowing, and with that, I am sure you will agree that a pleasant speech increases learning in both the speaker and the listener. To have understanding is like being a wellspring of life!

Pleasant words are as honeycomb, they are sweet to the mind and healing to the body!"

Jacob paused for a moment, looked at his wife with a gentle look and resumed talking saying_ "indeed, he who finds a true wife finds a good thing and obtains favor from the Lord."

"Oh! Oh! Oh! _Here comes November 27!" Lloyd said smiling and leading everyone into an outburst of laughter.

The Secret Behind Wisdom

The Secret Behind Wisdom

Ten

As the family was still laughing at the comment that Lloyd made, which was the wedding anniversary date of his parents, his mom went on to add_ "you know my son, as it is said, to everything there is a reason, and a time for every matter or purpose under heaven:

There is a time to be born and a time to die, a time to plant and a time to pluck up what is planted.

A time to kill and a time to heal, a time to break down and a time to build up,

A time to weep and a time to laugh, a time to mourn and a time to dance,

A time to cast away stones and a time to gather stones together, a time to embrace and a time to refrain from embracing,

A time to get and a time to lose, a time to keep and a time to cast away,

A time to rend and a time to sew, a time to keep silence and a time to speak,

A time to love and a time to hate, a time for war and a time for peace.

Hence the reason we confess that whatever God does, it endures forever; nothing can be added to it nor anything taken from it. And, the Why is so that men will reverently fear Him, revere and worship Him, knowing that He is the Great I Am."

"Maman, I love you very much and blessed that God blessed me to be yours and papa's child. I really mean it." Lloyd mentioned as he stood to hug his mother.

"We love you too dear son" she replied hugging him.

"Yes son" Jacob added, "children are the crown of old men, and the glory of children is their fathers.

It is said that bribe is like a bright, precious stone that dazzles the eyes and affects the mind of him who gives it; as if by magic he prospers, whichever way he turns.

When you cover and forgive an offense, you seek love, but the one who repeats or harps on a matter separates even close friends.

When you are a man of understanding, a reproof enters deeper into you than a hundred lashes into a self-confident fool.

Where I am going with this is that as a leader_ yes son, always look at it from a leader point of view. The beginning of strife is when water first trickles from a crack in a dam; therefore stop contention before it becomes worse and quarreling breaks out.

A person who loves conflicts and is quarrelsome loves wrongdoing and involves himself in guilt; the more a person raises his gateway and becomes boastful and arrogant simply invites self-destruction.

And for us parents, if we are the parents of a self-confident fool, the child does it to his sorrow, and the father has no joy in him.

Be happy always son! A happy heart is good medicine and a cheerful mind works healing, but a broken spirit dries up the bones.

As I have always told you Lloyd, a man of understanding sets skillful and godly wisdom before his face, but the eyes of self-confident fool are on the ends of the earth.

The Secret Behind Wisdom

A self-confident and foolish son is a grief to his father and bitterness to his mother, her who bore him.

No matter where you are, remember that the one who has knowledge spares his words, and a man of understanding has a cool spirit.

Today, if something happens and people are cursing, arguing, and whatever_ at that moment, even a fool when he holds his peace is considered wise; when he closes his lips he is esteemed a man of understanding. Therefore remember to be of a cool spirit."

The Secret Behind Wisdom

Eleven

As Jacob was talking, Lloyd stood and walked to the window in the living room that was overlooking the yard and whispered to himself, "I think I know now..." and went back to seat listening to his father's teachings.

"Son, death and life are in the power of the tongue, and those who indulge in it, eat the fruit of it.

As your father, I can give you houses and riches as inheritance, but a wise understanding and prudent wife will come from the Lord.

I am also proud to have you as a son because, you have done no violence to me, you have not chased your mother away because in doing so, it causes shame and brings reproach.

You may tell me that you try, but you should know that. Even a child is known by his acts, whether or not what he does is pure and right.

_And whoever curses his father or his mother, his lamp shall be put out in complete darkness, meaning his life shall go through many hustles and aches.

An advise I can ask you to keep dear in your heart and to pass on to the generations behind you is: beware of talebearers because a person like that will reveal secrets. Therefore, do not associate with those who talk too freely.

Remember, the one who guards his mouth and his tongue keeps himself from troubles."

Lloyds mum acknowledged the saying of her dear spouse and engaged with words of wisdom to her son. "Hearken to your father, who begot you and do not despise me when I get older.

Do not envy evil men, nor desire to be with them; because their minds plot oppression and devise violence, and their lips talk about causing trouble and vexation.

Through skillful and godly wisdom is a house, a life, a home, a family built, and by understanding it is established on a sound and good foundation,

And by knowledge shall every area of your life be filled with all precious and pleasant riches. With wise counsel you can wage your war, and in abundance of counselors there is victory and safety.

My dear son Lloyd, eat honey because it is good, and the drippings of the honeycomb are sweet to your taste.

So shall you know skillful and godly wisdom to be thus your life; if you find it, then there will be a future and a reward, and your hope and expectation shall not be cut off.

Do not lie in wait as a wicked man against the righteous; do not destroy their resting place. A righteous man can fall seven times and still rise again, but a wicked person, once they fall, they are overthrown by misfortune.

However, do not rejoice when your enemy falls, and do not let your heart be glad when he is overthrown.

When you do your evening prayer, recall these words: Ask the Lord to things; that He should not deny them to you before you die:

Remove far from you falsehood and lies; give you neither poverty nor riches; feed you with the food that needful for you because in case you are full and deny Him saying, who is the Lord?

Lloyd, no matter how much wealth, companies, cars, and whatever you may dream of you may have, There are four things which are little on earth, but they are exceedingly wise:

The ants are a people not strong, yet they lay up their food in the summer;

The conies are but a feeble folk, yet they make their houses in the rocks;

The locusts have no king, yet they go forth all of them by bands;

You can seize the lizard by your hands, yet it is also in kings' palaces.

_As a leader, as your father says. Learn to do right! Seek justice, relieve the oppressed, and correct the intimidator. Defend the fatherless, plead for the widow."

"You might wonder_" Jacob took over, "why your mother and I are giving you these words of wisdom and we somehow continuously link it to God. Well, it is written, man shall not live by bread alone, but by every word that comes forth from the mouth of God.

As your father, it is my duty to raise you well so that you grow socially, physically and spiritually. I may not give you all the spiritual knowledge you need, but I am not too worried because Blessed are the poor in spirit; for yours is the kingdom of heaven. When times are hard for you and that you mourn, I am still not worried because I know the Lord shall comfort you.

When opportunities come your way, and you don't jump at them instantly, but instead you are patient, meek, I am proud because I know that once again you are blessed because you shall inherit the wealth of the earth eventually!

Son, love your enemies and pray for those who harass you too. Take care not to do your good deeds publicly or before men, in order to be seen by them; otherwise you will have no reward with the Lord. So, whenever you give to the poor, do not blow a trumpet before you, as the hypocrites in the streets like to do that they may recognize and honor you by men.

You have a company with a lot of employees, and you meet a lot of people in your line of business.

Do not judge and criticize and condemn others, so that you may not be judged and criticized and condemned yourself. Life is simple, the way you judge, and criticize and condemn others, in accordance with the measure you use to deal out to others, it will be dealt out again to you.

Rejoice with those who rejoice, and weep with those who weep. Live in harmony with everyone around you; do not be snobbish, high minded, but readily adjust yourself to people and give yourself to humble tasks.

Never overestimate yourself or be wise in your own conceits. If your enemy is hungry, feed him; if he is thirsty, give him a drink; because when you do that, you will heap burning coals upon his head. Overcome the bad with good!"

Twelve

"Thank you papa for these words" Lloyd said with a smile on his face and continued saying, "after everything you've told me today, I don't know what we shall discuss during the road trip, how about we taking rain check on that one?"

"I knew it!" Lloyd's mum said in laughter as she left and began to make her way down to the basement.

"Well_ sure, we can take a rain check on the road trip and enjoy Ontario I guess!" Jacob responded to Lloyd.

"Thanks papa, by the way, I was talking with Tiffany the other day, and I was giving her a run down of your educational background, but realized I did not give her the details as to which institutions you attended_"

"Interesting, are you indirectly telling me that you don't know the institutions I attended_?"

"Nah, come on papa, of course I know the names of the institutions you attended, you graduated in medicine in 74, then you completed your Diagnostic Radiology Residency training in 78 and then you did an Advanced Clinical and Research Fellowship in Computed Tomography, Ultrasound, Neuroradiology, Interventional Radiology and Histomorphometry from 79 to 86; you also received a Ph.D. in Radiology in 86. I remember this one very well because I was there when you presented and it was a long day, but the party mum hosted at home was nice!"

"Hahaha_ you remember all that son?"

"I told you I know more in regard to all your grants and journal reviews and also the various countries where you went as a visiting professor."

"That is nice to know that my son has an interest in my career"

"Oh yeah, it's a career that I admire and deeply thank God for the blessing he gave you to be able to attain such heights and also thank God for having you as my father and mentor."

"Yes indeed, it is a blessing_ and as your father, I pray for you and your siblings every day so that the Lord may bless you more so you may do wonders for his glory"

"Thanks papa"

"No matter what you go through son, pray without ceasing! Put your trust and confidence in the Lord. You will face certain challenges in life, and those challenges shall not dissipate themselves with your intelligence, but it will be the kind that does not go out except by prayer and fasting.

It reminds me of the word in Ephesians that states _For I always pray to the God of our Lord Jesus Christ, the Father of glory, that He may grant you with a spirit of wisdom and revelation of insight into mysteries and secrets in the deep and intimate knowledge of Him, by having the eyes of your heart flooded with light, so that you can know and understand the hope to which He has called you, and how rich is His glorious inheritance in His set-apart ones.

And so that you can know and understand what is the immeasurable and unlimited and surpassing greatness of His power in and for us who believe, as demonstrated in the working of His mighty strength. _This scripture says it all son!"

"There is something that has helped me all along the way since the time I started high school until this day_ I would go to the book of psalms and whisper within my heart; Blessed are You, Oh Lord; teach me Your statutes.

Open my eyes that I may behold wondrous things out of Your law. My life dissolves and weeps itself away for heaviness; raise me up and strengthen me according to the promises of Your word.

Remove from me the way of the falsehood and unfaithfulness to You, and graciously impart Your law to me.

I will not merely walk, but run the way of Your commandments, when you give me a heart that is willing. Teach me, O Lord, the way of Your statutes, and I will keep it to the end. Give me understanding that I may keep Your law; yes, I will observe it with my whole heart.

The Secret Behind Wisdom

Turn away my eyes from beholding vanity; and restore me to vigorous life and health in Your ways. Establish Your word and confirm Your promise to Your servant, which is for those who reverently fear and devotedly worship you.

I long for your precepts; in Your righteousness give me a renewed life."

"My son, are you telling me that you literally have memorized psalm 119?"

"Well, memorized would be too much, but I have it well in my heart and meditate on it a lot_"

"Amen, keep going, I am listening son"

"_ I entreated Your favor with my whole heart; be merciful and gracious to me according to Your promise.

The Secret Behind Wisdom

At midnight I will rise to give thanks to You because of Your righteous ordinances.

Teach me good judgment, wise and right discernment, and knowledge, for I have believed, trusted, relied on Your commandments.

Let my mournful cry and supplication come before You, O Lord; give me understanding, discernment and comprehension according to Your word of assurance and promise.

Let my supplication come before You; deliver me according to Your word!

My lips shall pour forth praise with thanksgiving and renewed trust when You teach me Your statutes.

My tongue shall sing, praise for the fulfillment of Your word, for all Your commandments are righteous.

The Secret Behind Wisdom

Let Your hand be ready to help me, for I have chosen Your precepts.

Let me live that I may praise You, and let Your decrees help me."

"_That is the power you need son, by yourself you will never be able to successfully and truly accomplish the unthinkable. I am impressed and feel very blessed to see that you are placing the Lord Jesus in front of your every projects. I was once a young man like you and was also fortunate to be exposed to the word of God because without it, I don't think I would have been who I am today."

"Always trust in the Lord is what you told me Papa."

"My son, the reason I told you that is simply because those who trust in the Lord, those who lean on the Lord, and confidently hope in the Lord are like

Mount Zion, which cannot be moved, but abides and stands fast forever."

"Yes my son" Lloyds mum interrupted from the kitchen, "Extol the Lord always!"

"Extol, what does that exactly mean mum, I always see it, but don't quite understand what it means" Lloyd responded.

"Extol means to exalt, to praise, to worship. Hence, the reason we say I will extol You, my God, O King; and I will bless Your name forever and ever with grateful, affectionate praise."

"I see_ well my dear parents, I don't know how to thank you or if I will ever thank you enough for these words of love and wisdom. I am today the man that I am and I appreciate every single moment I spend with both of you.

I will make arrangements to fly back to the West Coast. I have been fully fed by the precious time we've spent together. I am more than ready once more to go out there and lead with the secrets of wisdom and leadership that you've given me over this marathon, if I can call it like that!"

"Hahaha, my son, you haven't stopped with those expressions of yours! That is good though, we are very blessed to have a son like you too and we shall continue to pray for you so that our Lord, our God, the God of Jacob, Isaac, David, Moses and Elijah may be by your side as you continue to try and better yourself to be a better man.

You have our blessing my son. We bless you and know that no weapon can be formed against you because you are an anointed child of the Lord."

The Secret Behind Wisdom

Thirteen

A few days went by, and Lloyd made his way back to Calgary.

"Tiffany!" Lloyd exclaimed himself as he entered the office

"Oh my God! Look at you all sparkling" Tiffany replied, "you must have finished all the food at your parents_ Hahaha"

"_Tell me about it!" said Lloyd

"So_ how was the trip? Come on spill, I'm listening" Tiffany said as she grabbed Lloyd by the arm into the staff lounge.

"It's long, very long, we need time to seat and talk." Lloyd responded as he poured himself a coffee.

Tiffany shook her head from side to side and engaged in conversation saying, "By the way, Lloyd I've never really understood the why of your quest for wisdom_"

"Wisdom is momentum, it's knowledge and it's power. Wisdom is a virtue! Without wisdom, not much can be accomplished, but yet lots can be destroyed" Lloyd replied as he sat at a table and inviting Tiffany to join him.

"I see, but the way you are thirsty for it Lloyd, there must be more to it_"

"Very true, there is a lot, it all started when I read proverbs 2. I have it here on my phone. Do you want me to read or you want to read it?" Lloyd asked his friend.

"You read, I am listening" Tiffany replied.

"Cool, here we go_" Lloyd said as he started to read "_My son, if you accept my words and store up my commands within you, turning your ear to wisdom and applying your heart to understanding—indeed, if you call out for insight and cry aloud for understanding, and if you look for it as for silver and search for it as for hidden treasure, then you will understand the fear of the Lord and find the knowledge of God.

For the Lord gives wisdom; from his mouth come knowledge and understanding. He holds success in store for the upright, he is a shield to those whose walk is blameless, for he guards the course of the just and protects the way of his faithful ones.

Then you will understand what is right and just and fair—every good path.

For wisdom will enter your heart, and knowledge will be pleasant to your soul. Discretion will protect you, and understanding will guard you.

The Secret Behind Wisdom

Wisdom will save you from the ways of wicked men, from men whose words are perverse, who have left the straight paths to walk in dark ways, who delight in doing wrong and rejoice in the perverseness of evil, whose paths are crooked and who are devious in their ways.

Wisdom will save you also from the adulterous woman, from the wayward woman with her seductive words, who has left the partner of her youth and ignored the covenant she made before God.

Surely her house leads down to death and her paths to the spirits of the dead. None who go to her return or attain the paths of life. Thus you will walk in the ways of the good and keep to the paths of the righteous.

For the upright will live in the land, and the blameless will remain in it; but the wicked will be cut off from the land, and the unfaithful will be torn from it."

"Interesting Lloyd_ and what's the rest" Tiffany said smiling.

"That is the beginning. You see, there are two kinds of wisdom! There is worldly and Godly wisdom. The one I thrive for is the Godly one.

If you read the first chapter in the book of Genesis of the Holy Bible, you will find that faith and wisdom were both introduced_ yes, you must be wondering how am I going from wisdom to faith now" Lloyd asked his friend.

"I am, but I will save my questions for when you are done" Tiffany responded.

"Sounds good_" Lloyd answered back and continued, "so, as I was saying, faith and wisdom were first introduced when you read in the book of Genesis and those two sources are still introduced today on a daily basis to our generation.

Actually, let me pull up a very interesting text that I fell upon while doing my research" Lloyd mentioned to Tiffany as he searched for the information on his Ipad.

"So if I may ask," Tiffany interrupted, "Is it better to have faith than wisdom?"

Lloyd looked at Tiffany, smiled and said, "I was torn between that question too and that is also why I went on to search so I could get an answer, but before you or I answer the question, remember there is Godly and worldly wisdom!"

"Fair enough" Tiffany responded.

"Here we go_ Satan is trying to get the people to accept his wisdom and pull them away from the faith that's in God's Word.

God is the Author of faith; Satan is the author of wisdom. For God gave His first children (Adam and Eve) His Word, and told them they must believe it yet Satan comes around and tries to offer Eve wisdom saying: "You will be wise, knowing right from wrong like God."

Wisdom comes from the devil. That's strange isn't it, but it's truth. Wisdom comes from the devil; he is the author of wisdom.

Now, of course anything that the devil has is a perversion of the original. Sin is a perversion of righteousness. Adultery is a perversion of a legal act. A lie is a perversion of the truth.

Now beware, there is the wisdom of God. The wisdom of God stays with His Word, but Satan in his wisdom tried to twist the Word; so that's the wisdom I'm speaking of.

There's a certain amount of faith that goes with Satan. In order to accept Satan you've got to believe Satan.

So there is a perverted faith to a perverted thing. And, anything that would try to twist the Word of God, to make it something that it doesn't, is the wrong spirit, offering wisdom against God's wisdom. So we're going to refer to it as wisdom and not Satan's faith.

The Bible says, the just shall live by faith, not what he can learn, but what he can believe. Wisdom has reasoning. Faith has no reasoning.

Check this - God is too good; God's too merciful; He loves you too much. You hear that same old devil today. God's too good to do this. God won't do this. God won't punish. He will do just exactly what His Word said He'd do. Satan is getting you to reason with him.

The moment you reason on God's Word, then you're losing faith.

There are so many people today that have the right knowledge that know that this Word should be God's Word, and it is God's Word; but they stand and let circumstances reason them out of it, away from the Holy Spirit, away from the things of God.

On the other hand, Faith has no reason; you don't reason at all; you believe. When you're prayed for and accept God's Word for healing, don't reason with your feelings. Don't reason with nothing else. There's no reasoning to it; God said so, and that settles it.

Faith simply trusts in the word of God. Trust his word. That is all God wants us to do. To trust in every Word He said. Some of them say, "Well, I believe this is true.

I believe that's true. I believe God can save, but I don't believe He can heal." That's the way they say it; having a form of godliness, but denying the Word thereof. Don't try to have wisdom; just believe the Word, have Faith and Godly wisdom will be given onto you.

Wisdom tries to reason and present a better way. Which is exactly what Satan told Eve: *Now, you're not going to die. Surely you won't, because God's a good God.*

If wisdom is with the Word, and proves to be with the Word, and the Word produces itself by the same thing, then it is the Word. But if wisdom is against the Word, and not with the Word, but trying to find something to add to it or take from it, it's of the devil.

I hope you are still following me?" Lloyd asked Tiffany.

"I am, it is clear, mostly when he says that we should not try to have wisdom, but just believe the word of God, and we shall be given Godly wisdom." Tiffany responded and continued by asking " but the thing I still don't quite understand, is_ and don't get offended by my question, but what makes you believe that with Godly wisdom you are pretty much golden?

I am asking that because I am not really a church or prayer person per se, but I am interested in knowing why_"

"I am not offended at all, and it is normal that you would want some clarity before you engage in it or before you fully adhere to it. The key to that is not to lean on our own understanding!" Lloyd responded calmly.

"Ok, Lloyd" Tiffany said laughing, "Please be more specific."

"I am serious, the key is not to lean on your own understanding. Let me read it for you here, he explains it further in the article here" Lloyd responded as he continued to read, "The Book of Proverbs, written by Solomon, who is one of the wisest men in the world, outside our Lord Jesus.

Solomon was just a man like us. He asked God for wisdom to run his kingdom. He was granted the gift of wisdom, the smartest man that we've ever known of outside our Lord.

In the Book of Proverbs the 3rd chapter reads –
My son, forget not my law; but let thine heart keep my commandments: For length of days, and long life, and peace, shall they add to thee.

Let not mercy and truth forsake thee: bind them about thy neck; write them upon the tables of thine heart. So shall thou find favour and good understanding in the sight of God and man.

The Secret Behind Wisdom

Trust in the LORD with all thine heart; and lean not unto thy own understanding. In all thy ways acknowledge him, and he shall direct thy path.

When, we are told not to lean on our own understanding, it does sound strange because the emphasis today is certainly laid upon education and upon our own understanding of things, the day of learning.

We send our children to school to have understanding. Then, after they are through with the grammar schools, we send them to high school for a better understanding of knowledge.

Then after they are through there, some children are even fortunate enough to go to college or university, and go through there to complete their education and their understanding of knowledge.

Yet, the wise Solomon told us not to lean to our own understanding; learn not of these things. We wonder why he would say such a thing as this, for it's because our modern understanding is usually the wisdom of man, which is contrary to the Word of God.

I think that's what Solomon was trying to advise his sons, he was not telling them to be illiterate, but not to lean to their understanding.

It's all right to have an education; there's nothing against that; but when that education is contrary to the Word of God, then lean to the Word and let your education go.

Education will stand and will give you a good job, probably a good standing amongst intellectual people, and, that's all right, which will probably be a great help to you, help you in your finances and your livelihood, make living maybe a little better for you.

But remember one thing, you've got to die. No matter how much education you got, and how much culture you are able to accumulate, you've yet got to face death because it is written, that man must die and after that the judgment.

Death is not so bad, but coming to the judgment is the bad part. Now, you can die, "but after that the judgment."

And God is not going to inquire of you how much schooling you got when you were here on earth, how much knowledge you accumulated, whether you've got your Bachelor of Art, or whatever degree you might have. It's not going to be required of you.

Your education is fine, but the Word of God is Life. "My Word is Life," and to know It is Life. And He said, "Know Him." He is the

Word. You can only know Him by the Word, for He is the Word. That's the only way you'll know Him, is by His Word.

Somebody could come up and say, "This is God," or "That's God," or "This is God," or "This is right," and "That's right," but we come back to the Word of God, which is the Truth. The Word of God is just like the-the North Star; it's a true star.

No matter which way the world's floating, that North Star is centered with the earth. You set your compass to the North Star. It's always in the center of the earth. Other stars float around with the world but the North Star stays stable.

Let us take a minute to consider some of those who did not lean on their own understanding; some characters of the

The Secret Behind Wisdom

Bible they did not lean on their own understanding, regardless of what the understanding of their era was.

Noah lived in a day of great scientific research. In the days of Noah they probably built pyramids cannot be reproduced. Now, we haven't got anything to do it, nothing to lift the rocks up there.

In those days, they had some kind of a chemical they could put in dye and make the clothes look natural until today. They had an embalming fluid that they could make a mummy; we could not make one today if we had to.

In the days of Noah, there was eating, drinking, marrying, and given in marriage; knew it not until Noah entered into the ark, and the flood come, taking all of them away.

Noah did not lean to his understanding.

It was a great scientific age, but he didn't lean to his understanding of his day. But he leaned on the promise of God, and moved by the power of God, and prepared an ark in the saving of His house, when it was absolutely contrary to common sense.

An ark built not with the knowledge and wisdom of Noah, but with the knowledge and wisdom of God.

There was no water up there, never had been. But he knew if God said there would be, there would be.

He leaned not to his own understanding, but by faith he moved by the Word of God's promise.

What if Moses had leaned to his own understanding, when God told him that he was to take the children of Israel out of Pharaoh's hand?

The Secret Behind Wisdom

What if he'd have leaned to his own understanding, when he was there by the Pillar of Fire, when God said, "Go down and I'll be with you"?

What if he'd had leaned to his understanding when he brought them to the Red Sea, and there they were at the water, and here God had promised them the promised land? What if he'd had leaned to his own understanding, "How am I going to get across there?

We don't have time to build a bridge. Here's the army coming right behind us. We have mountains on either side. Here the Red Sea in front of us"?

Now, if he'd leaned to his own understanding, he'd throw up his hands and run, fall at the feet of Pharaoh, and say, "Pharaoh, forgive me; I did wrong. I don't know what I was thinking." But he leaned not to his own understanding.

The Secret Behind Wisdom

He prayed, and God told him to step forward, and the sea opened up, which was against all reasoning's. But he leaned not to his own understanding.

Lean not to your own understanding. If you lean on your own understanding today when you're sick, maybe seating in a wheelchair, dying with cancer, heart trouble, and the doctor says you're going to die, if you lean to that understanding, you will die. But don't lean to that understanding.

That being said, there was one man who did lean to his own understanding, and his name was Judas Iscariot. I don't see how he could have done it. He'd walked face-to-face with Christ, just like Eve did in the beginning. He had seen the vindication; he'd looked at God in the face, like Eve did in the cool of the evening.

Eve looked at Christ in the cool of the evening in the garden.

Judas had set in the cool of the evening in the garden of Gethsemane and many places, and had looked at the same Christ; had heard Him teach, prove Himself by the Word, vindicated to be the prophet that Moses had spoken of would be raised up, and told them in the Scripture Who He was, and all about it. They had seen it proved by God, that He was, and then he leaned to his own understanding.

He leaned to his own understanding, instead of the understanding that that was the vindicated Word of God, and he did to Jesus just what the Scriptures said he would do.

Unfortunately, all this resulted in death, just like it did to Eve. And it does to all others who try to pervert the Word of God and lean to their own understanding.

Friend, don't lean upon reasons. Don't lean upon what you think, what somebody else thinks. By faith accept the promise of God. It isn't whether somebody else did it, whether they didn't do it, but what about you?

What will you do with this Jesus called the Christ, that makes Himself known in this day, the same as He did in that day?

In conclusion, a gift is not something for which you take a knife, and if you want to cut this with it, you can cut it; or you cut that, you can cut it, or whatever you want to. That's not a gift of God.

A gift of God is some way you have of getting yourself out of the way. Gifts and callings are the predestination of God.

"Gifts and callings are even without repentance." You're born with it, a little gear that you pull yourself over in, but you

The Secret Behind Wisdom

cannot step on the pedal. God has to operate it. You have to get yourself out of the way. Your faith can operate it, not mine, but yours."

"Well, well, well" Tiffany said as she stood to stretch, "I like the way he explains his stuff and how he shows that Godly wisdom can be awarded to each of us as long as we have faith in Jesus.

The thing is most people who are so into church stuff tend to send the message that everything else is worthless yet, this man clearly explains that it is important to be equally literate and get a good education and evolve in life, but not to let that get in the way of your faith because once you start doing things according to your own understanding things go down south."

"I agree with you" Lloyd answered.

The Secret Behind Wisdom

fourteen

"I still kind of don't quite understand the meaning of faith_ what is faith? Is it more like if I want something, I believe God will give it to me, and he will give to me if I have faith" Tiffany asked puzzled.

"In simple terms, Faith is not the belief that God will do what you want. It is the belief that God will do what is right." Lloyd answered.

"Sounds good, and what do you have to say about leadership?" Tiffany asked.

"In regard to leadership, there is also an interesting fact that I managed to dig while researching. If you think of it, each one of us, whether young or old, your first step that you ever made in your life, someone had to lead you.

Same as the last step you will ever make, someone will be leading you. In other words, someone always has to lead.

The first step you probably ever took in your life was probably the hands of a kind mother holding you. Your mother taught you how to walk, and you'd make a few steps and fall down, and get up, and you thought you were doing great things, then she turned you over to the schoolteacher. The teacher began to lead you to an education, of how and what you must do, and how you must learn, and so forth.

Then after the schoolteacher got through with you, you returned to your father. When your father got his turn, he taught you perhaps your business: how to be a successful businessman, how to do things right. Your mother taught you how to be a housewife, how to cook, and so forth like that.

The Secret Behind Wisdom

But the question now is, who leads you? You agree with me that we have to be led. No matter who we are here on earth, we are led."

"Yeah, I agree, but led by who" Tiffany responded.

Lloyd smiled and continued to explain to Tiffany "No matter how good you are, what you quit doing, what you start doing; you've got to accept the Person of the Lord Jesus Christ.

When you do that, He is the Word, and then your life fits right in the Word and it manifests itself to this age that you're living in. That's the best leader you can have!

You might tell me what about if you don't believe in Jesus ... what's in it for you! Well, The thing is, in life we have to confront things.

You are a mortal being and you're given the opportunity of choice.

You have a choice. God made it so you can choose. You can choose or reject. You have a choice.

You have a choice, as an individual, whether you're going to have an education or not. You have that choice. You can want to be or just not have it; you can just refuse it.

You have a choice of your conduct.

As a woman, you can look like a decent human being or you can be one of these weird creatures that we have out there, them blued eyes, and water-head haircuts and things; they are completely against the Word of God, which is absolutely contrary.

You can't mix the choice of your conduct; you're either for God or against God, and the outward expressions show exactly what's on the inside.

_ we have five senses that contact the outside body. God gave you five senses; not to contact Him, but for your earthly home: sight, taste, feel, smell, and hear.

Then you have a spirit on the inside of that, and it has five outlets: conscience, love, and so forth. There are five outlets that you use to contact the spirit world.

Your physical contacts the physical. Your spiritual contacts the spiritual. But inside you've got a soul, and that soul is that gene that came from God.

Like I was saying earlier, you have a choice of conduct. How you conduct yourself, that's up to you. Men have a choice of wife. We go out and take our wife. We take a wife, that's complementary to what we want, plan our future home to be.

Could you imagine a man, a Christian man, going out and taking one of these modern Jezebel for a wife? Could you imagine? What's the man thinking about?

What kind of a home is he going to have if he takes prostitute off of the street out here?

I can't stress it enough, but after all this research and reading, Leadership is the Holy Spirit. It leads you and guides you into all Truth.

Check Moses! He rejected the thrones and the popularity. He could have had women by the hundreds; think about it, Egypt ruled the world. The world lies right at his feet, and he was heir to every bit of it.

It doesn't matter how popular you could be, you could be a superstar; you could be a pastor; you could be a this, or that, or the other; but if that Word of Eternal Life by God's Word has been foreordained into you, and you see the thing at hand, it goes to work, moving you out like that.

It might cost you everything you got. It might cost you your home; it might cost you your friendship; it might cost you your stitch-and-sew party; it might cost you your place at the VIP events.

It might... I don't know what it'll cost you, but it'll cost everything that's worldly or pertains to the world. You will have to separate yourself from everything that's worldly. You will have to do it.

Moses laid everything aside and went into the desert with a stick in his hand. Days after days passed. Do you think he wondered if he thought he made a mistake? No! I don't think so.

Many times people start out, and they say,

"Oh, I can do it! Glory to God, I see it." And then they let somebody laugh at them and make fun of them, "Probably I was wrong."

It is said, "Those who cannot stand chastisement are bastard children and not the children of God." they're worked up on the emotion.

All of our societies, our church, our membership, and the things that we hold so dear, our American societies, and everything are very fine; there's nothing to be said against that.

There is no one denomination that can claim us, a true Christian, because you belong to God. Denominations are made by men, and Christianity is heaven sent.

But in all these things that we have, as good as they are, as fine as we come together, and as nice of meetings as we have, and social understanding that we have, yet we are each one confronted with Eternal Life.

No matter how successful we've been in business, or how successful we are, and what a great church member we are, and how we work, how we try to do things right, still if it's not done in the right way, it is a worship of God in vain."

"Lloyd, you seriously need to show me where I can find all these explanations_ like I've had so many question marks over the years and it has always been hard to understand. Thank you for this information." Tiffany replied.

The Secret Behind Wisdom

fifteen

Lloyd smiled and replied, "Tiffany, it has been a long journey. When you and my father spoke, it was clarifications and points of views I was getting from both of you.

I spent a lot of time reading the Holy Bible, and lots of time reading material related to Leadership, Faith and Wisdom in particular."

"I don't think I would be able to dedicate myself to doing that for so long pal" Tiffany said.

"I totally understand you Tiffany, I was there was once, but when your thirst begins, you will just go for it. When it hit me, I got the link with Psalm 42 vs 2 where it says_ My soul thirst for God, for the living God.

Tiffany, you get so thirsty that you end up wishing you could just meet Him face to face and have a talk and clarify all the questions and mysteries"

"Wow" Tiffany exclaimed herself, "It's for you man, I have been too notorious for that"

"Come on, don't say that" and Lloyd began to sing, "Jesus is For Everybody, Jesus is For Everybody.

Jesus Christ came for the notorious, and the saint.

Grace for the less glorious, and the fame.

Understand where the glory is, it's in His name."

"Nice, nice, I like the lyrics" Tiffany said.

"Yes, I like it too" Lloyd responded.

"Lloyd, seriously, I did not know you had all those skills in your back pocket! You should maybe write a book," Tiffany said with enthusiasm.

"Not a bad idea" Lloyd replied.

"Oh yeah, I meant to ask, what's this thing of breakthrough, I hear a lot of church people say that." Tiffany asked.

"To answer your question, as you know breakthrough means a sudden increase in knowledge, understanding, etc. in other words, an important discovery that happens after trying for a long time to understand or explaining something.

It is also described as a person's first important success. Hence the reason why you will hear the saying: You are the God of my breakthrough! Just as for my, acquiring godly wisdom is a breakthrough"

The Secret Behind Wisdom

"I see, I see. Any thoughts on the book ... yes ... no ... maybe? Tiffany asked laughing.

"A book on the subject of wisdom. This is how I will start a word form the author page:

Unlike an archaeologist who studies past cultures through artifacts, or items which people have made, used or modified. I am not.

These individuals do this to answer a specific research question or to save a cultural resource. As for me, I am a simple individual like you my reader. Thriving for a better today in hope of having a better tomorrow.

Acquiring knowledge to evolve in the right manner at the right pace has been on my heart for decades. If not since the day I knew I had to establish my legacy.

I was raised in a Christian family, and to date, I believe that the words in the holy Bible are true. It is the word of God. It is not a legend or a simple history book as some may say.

Why did I reference an archaeologist? Well, I have one thing in common with them. That is the research to answer a specific question.

The question on which I had been pondering for several months if not close to a year was: What is the secret behind godly wisdom?

I therefore decided to take a rather unusual approach. I asked those around me, I read books on leadership and I read my Bible more aggressively.

Wisdom is defined as the quality of having experience, knowledge, and good judgment; the quality of being wise.

The Secret Behind Wisdom

Godly wisdom is deeper and wiser! I decided, and I engaged myself into the quest. I decided to find and unveil the secret behind wisdom_ what do you think?" Lloyd asked.

"Well, my dear friend, you better start writing." Tiffany answered him as she nodded her head.

"I will get on it this weekend." Lloyd stated.

"You make reference to leadership books, to the Bible and other references, so are you telling me that in the Bible, they actually talk about the wisdom, black on white?" Tiffany asked with wondering face.

"The Holy Bible surely talks about wisdom, here let me show you_" Lloyd replied as he grabbed his iPad. And continued by reading "If any of you lacks wisdom, let him ask of God, who gives to all liberally and without reproach, and it will be given to him, (James 1:5)

And God gave Solomon wisdom and exceedingly great understanding, and largeness of heart like the sand on the seashore. (1 Kings 4:29)

That He would show you the secrets of wisdom! For they would double your prudence. Know therefore that God exacts from you Less than your iniquity deserves. (Job 11:16)

Wisdom is with aged men, And with length of days, understanding. (Job 12:12)

With Him are wisdom and strength, He has counsel and understanding. (Job 12:13)

No mention shall be made of coal or quartz, For the price of wisdom is above rubies. (Job 28:18)

And to man He said, 'Behold, the fear of the Lord, that is wisdom, And depart from evil is understanding."

The mouth of the righteous speaks wisdom, And his tongue talks of justice. (Psalm 37:30)

My mouth shall speak wisdom, And the meditation of my heart shall give understanding. (Psalm 49:3)

The fear of the Lord is the beginning of wisdom; A good understanding have all those who do His commandments. His praise endures forever. (Psalm 111:10)

Happy is the man who finds wisdom, And the man who gains understanding. (Proverbs 3:13)

Wisdom is the principal thing; Therefore get wisdom. And in all your getting, get understanding. (Proverbs 4:7)

"I, wisdom, dwell with prudence, And find out knowledge and discretion. (Proverbs 8:12)

When pride comes, then comes shame; But with the humble is wisdom. (Proverbs 11:2)

A man will be commended according to his wisdom, But he who is a perverse heart will be despised. (Proverbs 12:8)

And there is much, much more. If you take your time to search … you will find more"

"Sounds good, I will get into my bible so I can get some of that wisdom" Tiffany answered Lloyd as she made her way out towards the offices.

The Secret Behind Wisdom

Sixteen

If you are … then you should know that the Lord has located you … a true worshipper … those the Most High seeks … as David worshiped …

If you are one that bows down and asks for Mercy and Grace …

If you are one who would gladly give all you have …

Testify of His mightiness and elevate His name with a pure and sincere heart …

After Him, you follow and forsake all … Walk by faith and not by sight …

Subject yourself to the Lord …

Worship Him for He is The Great I Am …

The Secret Behind Wisdom

Rise up early in the morning and seek His face … Such is not just a word … such is the word …

All the ends of the earth shall remember and turn to the Lord, and all the families of the nations shall bow down and worship before the Lord …

The secret of the sweet, satisfying, companionship of the Lord have they who fear, revere and worship, the Lord, and He will show them His covenant and reveal to the them its deep, inner meaning.

For great is the Lord and gently to be praised; He is to be reverently feared and worshiped above all so-called gods.

O worship the Lord in the beauty of holiness; tremble before and reverently fear Him, all the earth.

Extol the Lord our God and worship at His

The Secret Behind Wisdom

footstool! Holy is He!

For as the heavens are high above the earth, so great are His mercy and loving-kindness toward those who reverently and worshipfully fear Him.

As a father loves and pities his children, so the Lord loves and pities those who fear Him with reverence, worship, and awe.

The Lord will fulfill his desires of those who reverently and worshipfully fear Him; He also will hear their city and will save them.

The reverent and worshipful fear of the Lord is the beginning and the principal and choice part of knowledge; its starting point and its essence; but fools despise skillful and godly wisdom, instruction, and discipline.

By worshipping, you will understand the

reverent and worshipful fear of the Lord and find the knowledge of our omniscient God.

Better is little with the reverent, worshipful fear of the Lord than great and rich treasure and trouble with it.

The reverent and worshipful fear of the Lord brings instruction in wisdom, and humility comes before honor.

...

Y, also referred as the second last letter of the occidental alphabet ...

The first letter of You ... the person of you.

Yes, it all begun with a why; And now known as the positive affirmation! Yes.

The beginning of wisdom ... the Lord is.

Most if not all, have wondered and asked ... Why are you the one and only true God?

The Secret Behind Wisdom

The creator of the Heaven and the Earth ...
The great I AM. You are.

The Secret Behind Wisdom

Seventeen

The day was almost reaching its end, when Tiffany hurried herself to Lloyd's office.

"Is everything okay" Lloyd asked as he could see the rather surprising expression on her face.

"I am fine" Tiffany responded as she took a seat on the couch by the window. "Lloyd, have you ever heard of the beatitudes?"

"Yes, I have, they are quite a piece of_"

And before Lloyd cold be done his sentence, Tiffany interrupted, "talk no more and listen to this, it's from a book one of my girls sent me via kindle share."

"Sure, go ahead I am listening." Lloyd responded to her.

"Perfect, listen and please don't interrupt until I am done." Tiffany mentioned as she began to read. "Melchizedech, King of Righteousness. If only humanity used the beatitudes...

I am the one who no one speaks of, yet I was there ... I walked, ate, slept and heard Him. Was it wrong what I did at the time or was it something that I was doing without knowing that one-day harvest will come and find me.

The long days and nights of walking from village to village, town-to-town and city-to-city ... Interestingly, it never seemed worthless. Something inside me, kept telling me to continue following and not to miss a single moment if not only when I'd blink my eyes to confirm to me that I was not dreaming nor letting my imagination be creative, but that I was indeed leaving the moment at the instant.

My first encounter with him was in Jordan. I was there on the hill overlooking the Jordan River. John the Baptist was there and as usual he was doing what he had been doing for quite a number of years, he was preaching in the wilderness of Judea and saying _ Repent, for the kingdom of heaven has come near.

Nevertheless, that day felt different, it was a day unlike any other day. Despite the shining sun and the heat, it felt right to be outside, not even under a shadow, but just to be there and observe the scenery. The banks of the river were busy with a crowd lined up to go and get baptized by John the Baptist.

The fascinating thing about John the Baptist, was his striking voice … I could hear it all the way from the top of the hill. His attire was not the common one that one would expect, his clothes were made of camel's hair, and he had a leather belt around his waist. From what I heard, his diet was not a conventional one either, his food was locusts and wild honey; but be not fooled; he was very strong and healthy!

Everything was going as it always went when John the Baptist did his water baptism, until, a Man stood in front of him. John stopped and I could tell there was a dialogue between the two.

Thereafter, John the Baptist baptized him, the Man turned around and began to make his way up the hill. He continued to walk and soon all we could see was his silhouette.

That's when I began to run and follow Him to see where he was going because at that moment … it became a mystery to me …

I wondered who was this individual that I

had never seen in the area … where did he come from and where was he going and what was his purpose?

Some forty days and forty nights had passed; I had lost sight of this Man, until the day came …

There I was again, on a calm day, resting by the lake in the area of Zebulun and Naphali when I heard someone say_ Repent, for the kingdom of heaven has come near.

I jumped to my feet, thinking it was John the Baptist that I had not seen in ages, but no, it was that Man, who John the Baptist had baptized that day in the Jordan River. That is when I decided to follow him and see exactly who he was. He was the first person I heard repeating those words!

The journey commenced near the Sea of Galilee. He approached two men who seemed to be brothers and told them _ Come, follow me, and I will send you out to fish for people.

These two, listened to him and began to walk with Him. As for me, I was also following them and listening to this Man, who kept intriguing me. I kept asking myself, what kind of Man is he?

As he continued to walk, the crowds continued to grow and grow and, he would heal the paralyzed, those having seizures, those suffering from severe pain, those with various diseases and I believe even those the demon possessed.

A day came, his main followers, or His disciples if I may refer to them like that, surrounded him and he began to give them beatitudes saying _ Blessed are the poor in spirit, for theirs is the kingdom of heaven.

Blessed are those who mourn, for they will be comforted. Blessed are the meek, for they will inherit the earth.

Blessed are those who hunger and thirst for righteousness, for they will be filled. Blessed are the merciful, for they will be shown mercy.

Blessed are the pure in heart, for they will see God. Blessed are those who are persecuted because of righteousness for theirs is the kingdom of heaven.

Blessed are you when people insult you, persecute you and falsely say all kinds of evil against you because of me. Rejoice and be glad, because great is your reward in heaven, for in the same way they persecuted the prophets who were before you.

I realized that He was an eloquent speaker. He spoke with passion and power.

His preachings were not just mere arrangements of words, but you could feel the wisdom and the purity.

As He continued to teach his disciples he said_ You are the salt of the earth. But if the salt loses its saltiness, how can it be made salty again? It is no longer good for anything, except to be thrown out and trampled underfoot.

You are the light of the world. A town built on a hill cannot be hidden. Neither do people light a lamp and put it under a bowl. Instead they put it on its stand, and it gives light to everyone in the house.

In the same way, let your light shine before others, that they may see your good deeds and glorify your Father in Heaven.

When I heard those words, I was amazed and felt like a different being, but again was wondering how will the law be fulfilled if he says that, and that is when I heard him saying_ Do not think that I have come to abolish the Law or the Prophets: I have not come to abolish them but to fulfill them.

For truly I tell you, until heaven and earth disappear, not the smallest letter, not the least stroke of a pen, will by any means disappear from the Law until everything is accomplished.

Therefore anyone who sets aside one of the least of these commands and teaches others accordingly will be called least in the Kingdom of heaven, but whoever practices and teaches these commands will be called great in the kingdom of heaven.

For I tell you that unless your righteousness surpasses that of the Pharisees and the teachers of the law, you will certainly not enter the Kingdom of heaven.

In those days, murder, adultery, divorce, taking oath, treating people eye for eye and tooth for tooth, hating our enemies, and not sharing with the needy was very common.

Yet no one had taken the time to address these issues and help people understand the law. Unlike, all the others, this mysterious man of mine addressed it saying_ You have heard that it was said to the people long ago, 'You shall not murder, and anyone who murders will be subject to judgment. But I tell you that anyone who is angry with a brother or a

The Secret Behind Wisdom

sister will be subject to judgment. Again, anyone who says to a brother or sister, Raca, is answerable to the court. And anyone who says, 'You fool!' will be in danger of the fire of hell.

Therefore, if you are offering your gift at the altar and there remember that your brother or sister has something against you, leave your gift there in front of the altar. First go and be reconciled to them; then come and offer your gift.

Settle matters quickly with your adversary who is taking you to court. Do it while you are still together on the way, or your adversary may hand you over to the judge, and the judge may hand you over to the officer, and you may be thrown into prison. Truly I tell you, you will not get out until you have paid the last penny.

You have heard that it was said, 'You shall not commit adultery' But I tell you that anyone who looks at a woman lustfully has already committed adultery with her in his heart. If your right eye causes you to stumble, gouge it out and throw it away. It is better for you to lose one part of your body than for your whole body to be thrown into hell.

And if your right hand causes you to stumble, cut it off and throw it away. It is better for you to lose one part of your body than for your whole body to go into hell.

It has been said, 'Anyone who divorces his wife must give her a certificate of divorce.' But I tell you that anyone who divorces his wife, except for sexual immorality, makes her the victim of adultery, and anyone who marries a divorced woman commits adultery.

It was amazing how each time questions arose in my mind… he would address it like he could hear me.

_Again, you have heard that it was said to the people long ago, 'Do not break your oath, but fulfill to the Lord the vows you have made. But I tell you, do not swear an oath at all, either by heaven, for it is God's throne; or by earth, for it is his footstool; or by Jerusalem, for it is the city of the Great King.

And do not swear by your head, for you cannot make even one hair white or black. All you need to say is simply 'Yes' or 'No', anything beyond this comes from the evil one.

You have heard that it was said, 'Eye for eye, and tooth for tooth.' But I tell you, do not resist an evil person. If anyone slaps you on the right cheek, turn to them the other cheek also.

The Secret Behind Wisdom

And if anyone wants to sue you and take your shirt, hand over your coat as well. If anyone forces you to go one mile, go with them two miles.
Give to the one who asks you, and do not turn away from the one who wants to borrow from you.

You have heard that it was said, 'Love your neighbor and hate your enemy. But I tell you, love your enemies and pray for those who persecute you, that you may be children of your Father in heaven. He causes his sun to rise on the evil and the good, and sends rain on the righteous and the unrighteous.

If you love those who love you, what reward will you get?
Are not even the tax collectors doing that? And if you greet only your own people, what are you doing more than others?

Do not even pagans do that? Be perfect, therefore, as your heavenly Father is perfect.

Be careful not to practice your righteousness in front of others to be seen by them. If you do, you will have no reward from your Father in heaven.

So when you give to the needy, do not announce it with trumpets, as the hypocrites do in the synagogues and on the streets, to be honored by others.

Truly I tell you, they have received their reward in full. But when you give to the needy, do not let your left hand know what your right hands is doing, so that your giving may be in secret. Then your father, who sees what is done in secret, will reward you.

This Man, was always passionate and always took time to explain things in a way that you wanted to run out there and instantly do what He said, but again you wanted to stay and continue following and listening so you did not miss another interesting thing he'd say or do. Just like the day he spoke of prayer.

He said_ And when you pray, do not be like the hypocrites, for they love to pray standing in the synagogues, and on the street corners to be seen by others.

Truly I tell you, they have received their reward in full. But when you pray, go into your room, close the door and pray to your Father, who is unseen.

Then your Father, who sees what is done in secret, will reward you. And when you pray, do not keep on babbling like pagans, for they think they will be heard because of their many words. Do not be like them, for your Father knows what you need before you ask him.

The Secret Behind Wisdom

This, then, is how you should pray:

'Our father in heaven, hallowed be your name, your kingdom come, you will be done, on earth as it is heaven.

Give us today our daily bread. And forgive us our debts, As we also have forgiven our debtors.

And lead us not into temptation, But deliver us from the evil one.

For if you forgive other people when they sin against you, your heavenly Father will also forgive you. But if you do not forgive others their sins, your Father will not forgive your sins.

    I had always heard people say that they prayed. Some would say it is when they talk to God. Prayer was something that had always intrigued me. Yet, no one had ever taken the time to teach another prayer. In part, I was to blame, I never took the time to ask how it was done …

I assumed it was something that comes with you, either you have it or you don't. The individual that I was, anything to do with belief was a too much time. It was profitless, would not make me any stronger, nor would it make me more successful.

Despite the fact that the back of my mind always wondered why some individual, some people, some nation would give it so much importance and reverence …

I made it a must push it away. It made no sensible sense that a so-called prayer could take care of me or anyone else for that matter.

These thoughts were all storming back in my mind as I was observing the Man with his followers talk.

It was getting so overwhelming until I managed to refocus on what He was saying and heard him say_

When you fast, do not look somber as the hypocrites do, for they disfigure their faces to show others they are fasting.

Truly I tell you, they have received their reward in full. But when you fast, put oil on your head and wash your face, so that it will not be obvious to others that you are fasting, but only to your Father, who is unseen; and your Father, who sees what is done in secret, will reward you.

Do not store up for yourselves treasures on earth, where moths and vermin destroy, and where thieves break in and steal. But store up for yourselves treasures in heaven, where moths and vermin do not destroy, and where thieves do not break in and steal. For where your treasure is, there your heart will be also.

The eye is the lamp of the body. If your eyes are healthy, your whole body will be full of light. But if your eyes are unhealthy, your whole body will be full of darkness. If then the light within you is darkness, how great is that darkness!

No one can serve two masters. Either you will hate the one and love the other, or you will be devoted to the one and despise the other. You cannot serve both God and money.

And there was my issue, this man that I had begun to admire and to some extent believe in, would throw at me truths that would pierce my heart and make me wonder, what good is it for me to continue with my life. How dare He tell me not to worry while there was so much uncertainty everywhere one would go!

The Secret Behind Wisdom

But to him, it did not seem to matter how much uncertainty one could have, not that he did not care, but he was actually reassuring those with whom He was talking and to me the unknown follower. He was so calm and confident with every word He mentioned

_Therefore I tell you, do not worry about your life, what you will eat or drink; or about your body, what you will wear. Is not life more than food, and the body more than clothes?

Look at the birds of the air; they do not sow or reap or store away in barns, and yet your heavenly Father feeds them. Are you not much more valuable than they? Can any one of you by worrying add a single hour to your life?

And why do you worry about clothes? See how the flowers of the field grow. They do not labor or spin.

The Secret Behind Wisdom

Yet I tell you that not even Solomon in all his splendor was dressed like one of these.

If that is how God clothes the grass of the field, which is here today and tomorrow is thrown into the fire, will he not much more clothe you-you of little faith?

So do not worry, saying, 'What shall we eat?" or 'What shall we drink?" or 'what shall we wear?'

For the pagans run after all these things, and your heavenly Father knows that you need them. But seek first his kingdom and his righteousness, and all these things will be given to you as well.

Therefore do not worry about tomorrow, for tomorrow will worry about itself. Each day has enough trouble of its own.

The Secret Behind Wisdom

Faith! That was the word. During my walks I had overheard one say that faith is confidence in what we hope for and assurance about what we do not see.

This is what the ancients were commended for.
By faith we understand that the universe was formed at God's command, so that what is seen was not made out of what was visible.

By faith Abel brought God a better offering than Cain did. By faith he was commended as righteous, when God spoke well of his offerings. And by faith Abel still speaks, even though he is dead.

By faith Enoch was taken from this life, so that he did not experience death. He could not be found, because God had taken him away. For before he was taken, he was commended as one who pleased God. And without faith it is impossible to please God, because anyone who comes to him must believe that he exists and that he rewards those who earnestly seek him.

By faith Noah, when warned about things not yet seen, in holy fear built an ark to save his family. By his faith he condemned the world and became heir of the righteousness that is in keeping with faith.

By faith Abraham, when called to go to a place he would later receive as his inheritance, obeyed and went, even though he did not know where he was going.

By faith he made his home in the promised land like a stranger in a foreign country; he lived in tents, as did Isaac and Jacob, who were heirs with him of the same promise.

The Secret Behind Wisdom

For he was looking forward to the city with foundations, whose architect and builder is God. And by faith even Sarah, who was past childbearing age, was enabled to bear children because she considered him faithful who had made the promise.

And so from this one man, and he as good as dead, came descendants as numerous as the stars in the sky and as countless as the sand on seashore.

By faith Isaac blessed Jacob and Esau in regard to their future. That was the faith level I wanted to attain, but I needed more direction and understanding of certain principles.

I was determined to seek and I knew eventually I would find. The same way I encountered this Man that day.

It felt strange and stranger, days, weeks, months passed by and it was getting deeper. He was answering some questions I had always had and some questions that were coming up as he was talking.

I could see the same expression on his followers' faces as he spoke_ Do not judge, or you too will be judged. For in the same way you judge others, you will be judged, and with the measure you use, it will be measured to you.

Why do you look at the speck of sawdust in your brother's eye and pay no attention to the plank in your own eye? How can you say to your brother, 'Let me take the speck out of your eye,' when all the time there is a plank out of your own eye, and then you will see clearly to remove the speck from your brother's eye.

Do not give what is sacred; do not throw your pearls to pigs. If you do, they may trample them under their feet, and turn and tear you to pieces.

Despite all he said, I never doubted him for a minute; his words were bringing peace and confidence. The will and ambition of becoming a better citizen was slowly starting to become an attainable target. He would speak in parables at times that could be a bit hard to follow, but when it was all said and done, it was clear in my mind.

I knew and understood and was looking forward to more. My quest was more than a treasure hunt because it was all there given to me and easy to digest.

He resumed saying_ Ask and it will be given to you; seek and you will find; knock and the door will be opened to you. For everyone who asks receives; the one who seeks finds; and to the one who knocks, the door will be opened.

Which of you, if your son asks for bread, will give him a stone? Or if he asks for a fish, will give him a snake?

If you, then, though you are evil, know how to give good gifts to your children, how much more will your Father in heaven give good gifts to those who ask him! So in everything, do to others what you would have them do to you, for this sums up the Law and the Prophets.

At times, I felt like shouting with joy, or clap my hands, just do something ... it felt so sweet, but His calm, gentleness and demeanor would embrace me and I kept thirsting for more as he spoke wisdom and knowledge_ Enter through the narrow gate. For wide is the gate and broad is the road that leads to destruction, and many enter through it. But small is the gate and narrow the road that leads to life, and only few find it.

The Secret Behind Wisdom

Was I considered one of those? I hope not, and even if I was … I felt better because now I knew what to do and how to do it. I knew what to be aware of whether it was true or false. He was saying it all … it was like the heavens were opened and granted access to everyone who wanted in.

This Man looked at his followers and said_ "Watch out for false prophets. They come to you in sheep's clothing, but inwardly they are ferocious wolves. By their fruit you will recognize them.

Do people pick grapes from thornbushes, or figs from thistles? Likewise, every good tree bears good fruit, but a bad tree cannot bear good fruit.

Every tree that does not bear good fruits is cut down and thrown into the fire. Thus, by their fruit you will recognize them.

Crowds including myself were always amazed at the teachings He gave. It was authority in order and due time.

A day came when he sent out His twelve disciples. It was a sad and happy day for me. It felt like a graduation ceremony. They were well prepared and as they got ready to take the road, he gave them valuable instructions that were heartwarming, saying_ Do not go among the Gentiles or enter any town of the Samaritans. Go rather to the lost sheep of Israel.

As you go, proclaim this message: 'The kingdom of heaven has come near.' Heal the sick, raise the dead, cleanse those who have leprosy, drive out demons. Freely you have received, freely give.

Do not get any gold or silver or copper to take with you in your belts- no bag for the journey or extra shirt or sandals or a staff, for the worker is worth his keep. Whatever town or village you enter, search there for some worthy person and stay at their house until you leave.

As you enter the home, give it your greeting. If the home is deserving, let your peace rest on it; if it is not, let your peace return to you. If anyone will not welcome you or listen to your words, leave that home or town and shake dust off your feet.

Truly I tell you, it will be more bearable for Sodom and Gomorrah on the day of judgment than for that town.

I am sending you out like sheep among wolves. Therefore be as shrewd as snakes and as innocent as doves.

Be on your guard: you will be handed over to the local councils and be flogged in the synagogues. On my account you will be brought before governors and kings as witnesses to them and to the gentiles.

But when they arrest you, do not worry about what to say or what to say or how to say it. At that time you will be given what to say, for it will not be you speaking, but the Spirit of your Father speaking through you.

Brother will betray brother to death, and a father his child; children will rebel against their parents and have them put to death. You will be hated by everyone because of me, but the one who stands firm to the end will be saved. When you are persecuted in one place, flee to another. Truly I tell you, you will not finish going through the towns of Israel before the Son of Man comes.

The student is not above the teacher, nor a servant above his master. It is enough for students to be like their teachers, and servants like masters. If the head of the house has been called Beelzebul, how much more the members of his household!

So do not be afraid of them, for there is nothing concealed that will not be disclosed, or hidden that will not be made known. What I tell you in the dark, speak in the daylight: what is whispered in your ear, proclaim from the roofs. Do not be afraid of those who kill the body but cannot kill the soul.

Rather, be afraid of the One who can destroy both soul and body in hell. Are not two sparrows sold for a penny? Yet not one of them will fall to the ground outside your Father's care. And even the very hairs of your head are all numbered. So don't be afraid; you are worth more than many sparrows.

The Secret Behind Wisdom

Whoever acknowledges me before others, I will also acknowledge before my Father in heaven. But whoever disowns me before others, I will disown before my father in heaven.

Do not suppose that I have come to bring peace to earth. I did not come to bring peace, but a sword.

For I have come to turn a man against his father, a daughter against her mother, a daughter-in-law against her mother-in-law. A man's enemies will be the members of his own household.

Anyone who loves their father or mother more than me is not worthy of me; anyone who loves their son or daughter more than me is not worthy of me.
Whoever does not take up their cross and follow me is not worthy of me. Whoever finds their life will lose it, whoever loses their life for my sake will find it.

The Secret Behind Wisdom

Anyone who welcomes you welcomes me, and anyone who welcomes me welcomes the one who sent me. Whoever welcomes a prophet as a prophet will a prophet's reward, and whoever welcomes a righteous person as a righteous person will receive a righteous person's reward. And if anyone gives even a cup of cold water to one of these little ones who is my disciple, truly I tell you, that person will certainly not lose their reward.

Wow!
I whispered ... I knew I was in the presence of not just anybody that claimed to be somebody; but I was in the presence of Melchizedek, I had been walking with Jesus.

Yes, it was He! Jesus Christ, the Messiah, the Anointed, the son, the descendant of David, the son, the descendant of Abraham.

It was not long after, he was crucified ... but he never stayed there, He rose. Yes, He has risen!

The day Jesus rose, he said to his disciples_ All the authority in heaven and on earth has been given to me.

Therefore, go and make disciples of all nations, baptizing them in the name of the Father and of the Son and of the Holy Spirit, and teaching them to obey everything I have commanded you. And surely I am with you always, to the very end of the age.

As the words began to consume me, the echoes of His word became aloud and alive. It became a personal conversation ... the beatitudes began to echo in me ...

I then thought I was ready to go begin the journey of life ... but there I was seated ...

and I heard a voice saying: As you go, remember all these promises ...

It was like someone was going through a manuscript, and was decreeing_ I am the Lord your God and I never change.

I am full of mercy and grace and I overflow with love.

The intentions of My heart will remain steadfast forever.

I created you in My own image with My special blessing.

I chose you to be adopted into My family before creation.

I delivered you from darkness into the kingdom of My beloved Son.

I have given you eternal life because you have believed in Jesus Christ.

The Secret Behind Wisdom

I sent the Spirit of My Son into your heart so you could call Me Father.

Since you are in Christ, I have made you an heir of all My Promises.

I have given you a new heart and put My own Spirit in you.

My plan for your future is filled with hope.

I am at work in your life through the desires of your heart.

I will give you rest in green pastures and lead you to still waters.

I give My Spirit in unlimited measure.

I will take hold of your hand to keep you from falling.

I will provide every good thing you need to do My will.

I will discipline you in love as a father who loves his children.

My power will rest on you when you are weak.

I will bless your life and keep watch over you always.

If you search for Me with all your heart, you will find Me.

I will shield your life and deliver you from the wicked.

Cast all your worries on Me, for I really care about you.

I will not let you be tested beyond what you can endure.

The Secret Behind Wisdom

My love will persevere through every situation.

I will not withhold anything good from those with an upright heart.

I look after foreigners and I help the fatherless and the widow.

I will guard those who have a childlike heart.

You are more than a conqueror through My love in Jesus Christ.

When Jesus appears, you will receive a crown of glory that will never dim.

At the end of the age, My righteous ones will shine like the sun in My kingdom.

Not one of My promises will ever fail you.

The Secret Behind Wisdom

I am seated in the heavens and My kingdom reigns over all.

All my plans will be fulfilled, for I know the end from the beginning.

I knew you before you were born and I designed you for my purpose.

You are holy and free from blame because of Jesus Christ's death.

I have blotted out your sins and dissolved them like the mist.

I have sealed you with My Spirit to guarantee your coming inheritance.

I will be a real Father to you.

I will look after you and teach you the way that is best.

Trust in Me with all your heart and I will guide you.

I will give you peace at all times and in every situation.

I am your shelter and a place of safety from your enemies.

If you wait for Me, I will work on your behalf.

My love will never fail you.

I am your Shepherd and I will meet all your needs.

I will keep you safe because no one can snatch you out of My hand.

I will heal your broken heart and mend all your wounds.

The Secret Behind Wisdom

I will bless you in times of mourning with My comfort.

You will find freedom wherever My Spirit dwells.

You can know and depend on the love that I have for you.

You can trust in Me for I will never forsake you.

I put people who are lonely in families

I hear you when you ask for anything according to My will.

I will reward those who diligently seek me with a heart of faith.

I will sanctify you and keep you blameless until Jesus returns.

The Secret Behind Wisdom

When your body fails, you have an eternal home waiting for you.

Those who overcome will sit with My Son on His throne.

My promise of life is for you and your family.

The earth belongs to Me and all that is in it.

My throne will stand forever and justice will reign in My kingdom.

The grass will dry up and flowers will fall, but My Word will endure forever.

Though the mountains vanish, My unending love will never leave you.

I have called you out of darkness into My glorious light.

The Secret Behind Wisdom

I have chosen the weak things of this world to confound the strong.

I delight to reveal My kingdom to those with a childlike heart.

I have brought you close through the blood of Christ.

Your old life has died and your new life is hid with Christ in Me.

The same Spirit that raised Jesus from the dead will also give life to you.

I have blessed you in Christ with every heavenly blessing.

I had not realized for how long I had been there listening to this calm voice that came out with authority.

_ Commit all that you do to Me and your plans will be successful.

The Secret Behind Wisdom

I am with you and I will help you because I am your God.

I will never abandon you.

I see all your hardships and I care about your suffering.

When you pass through turbulent waters, I will be close to you.

My anointing will teach you all you need to know.

If you live My secret place, you will find rest under My shadow.

I will give you My strength to help you stand in high places.

Thousands may fall around you, but you will not be harmed.

The Secret Behind Wisdom

I provide food for the hungry and justice for the oppressed.

My divine power will give you all you need to live a good life.

My mercy will overrule judgment.

I will cause all things to ultimately work for your good.

Humble yourself before Me and in time I will exalt you.

I have carved your name in the palms of My hands.

Never tire of doing good, for in time you will reap a harvest.

An eternal crown awaits you t the finish line, so keep running your race.

I prepared a kingdom inheritance for you when I created the world.

It is precious for Me to see My faithful ones come home.

I will protect and carry you all the days of your life.

I will restore and refresh your weary soul.

I will always build you up, not pull you down.

If you make your home in Me, then no evil will come your way.

If you delight in My word, you will be fruitful and prosperous.

I will cover you all day long as you rest between My shoulders.

Come close to Me and I will come close to you.

My gentleness will enlarge your life.
Ask Me for wisdom and I will generously give it to you.

I will give you power to know the vastness of My immeasurable love.

Wait patiently for Me and I will hear your cry.

Even when you are weak in your faith, I will remain faithful to you.

Seek My kingdom first and everything you need will be given to you.

My Spirit will lead you into all truth and show you what is to come.

One day, I will wipe away every tear and take away all your pain.

The Secret Behind Wisdom

My everlasting joy and gladness will drive all sorrow and mourning away.

All your days are known to Me and your inheritance is secure forever.

My face will shine upon you all the days of your life.

My Word will brighten your steps and light your path.

My son took upon Himself all your sicknesses and diseases.

My Spirit will help you in your weakness.

You can do all things through Jesus Christ who gives you strength.

Be courageous, for I am with you and I will never fail you.

I am a very present help for you in times of trouble.

I will keep watch over you and guard you forever.

I hear your voice when you call to Me in the morning.

I will teach Your children My ways and give them great peace.

I will not forget the love you have shown Me by serving others.

I will repay those who are kind to the poor.

All My blessings will overtake those who obey Me.

I will rescue the godly from all their troubles.

My displeasure may last a moment, but My favor is yours for life.

I will show you the mysteries of My kingdom.

I began the good work in you and I will finish it.

My Word will not return to Me until it accomplishes what I intended.

I will not abandon you, for I am glad to make you My very own.

I have removed your sins from you as far as the east is from the west.

You can enjoy freedom because Christ has set you free.

I have anointed you with My Spirit as a down payment of what is yet to come.

Every good gift that you receive comes directly form My hand.

Nothing will be impossible for those who have even a little faith.

Call out to me and I will show you wonderful things you do not know.

I will reveal My secrets to those who fear Me.

I am able to do more for you than you could possibly imagine.

When you walk through the fires of adversity, you will not be burned.

No weapon created for your harm will succeed against you.

My Spirit will rest upon you when you suffer for Christ's sake.

My goodness will lead you to a change of heart.

I will bless the peacemakers and call them My children.

I will protect the fatherless and widows can trust in Me.

I am a father to the fatherless and I defend the cause of widows.

I will provide justice for everyone who is mistreated.

My name is a strong tower that you can run to and find safety.

If you persist and do My will, you will receive what I have promised.

I am faithful to keep My covenant of kindness to a thousand generations.

The Secret Behind Wisdom

I will not abandon My own inheritance.

I am the Lord your God who heals all of your diseases.

I forgive sins and I love to show mercy.

I will meet your every need through My eternal riches in Jesus Christ.

Do not be sad, for My joy is your strength.

My perfect love will banish fear from your heart.

I will save you in the midst of your troubles.

I will blanket My protection over all who trust in Me.

My armor will help you stand against the plans of the enemy.

I will turn your mourning into dancing and surround you with joy.

I will restore your health and heal all your hurts.

I will strengthen you with feet like a deer so you can reach great heights.

If you share with the needy, My glory will guard your back.

If you enter into My rest, you will find rest from all your striving.

I am near to you whenever you cry out.

When problems arise, call to Me and I will answer you.

Don't worry, I will take care of you.

Those who overcome will be made pillars in My temple forever.

The Secret Behind Wisdom

You can trust in My faithfulness

I am good and My mercy is everlasting.

If you walk in the light, the blood of My Son Jesus will cleanse you from all sin.

Trust in Me, and do not be afraid of what others can do to you.

Forgiveness and healing are among My many benefits.

If you rest in Me and wait patiently, you will inherit the land.

I give power to the exhausted and I strengthen the weak.

If I am for you, no one can stand against you.

Though you have many plans, My purpose will be fulfilled.

If two of you agree in prayer, I will do whatever you ask.

I will make you fruitful in your old age.

Do not despise My discipline, for in time, I will heal your wounds.

I will comfort you just like a mother would. Your sadness may last for a night, but joy will come in the morning.

I will sow mercy to those who are merciful to others.

I bless My righteous ones and shield them with My favor.

I will anoint you with oil, so your cup overflows.

My thoughts toward you outnumber the sand on the seashore.

I will give you a double portion of your inheritance in exchange for your shame.

I will be the voice behind you, guiding you in the way you should go.

I will train you for battle with My shield of salvation.

I will be faithful to give you My strength and protection.

You will find safety in My everlasting arms. I carry your burdens every day.

I have called you to inherit My blessing.

If you honor Me with your firstfruits, you will overflow with abundance.

If you help the poor, your light will shine like the dawn.

If you wait for Me, I Will renew your strength.

I will give you a peaceful sleep surrounded by safety.

I will enrich your life and renew your youth like the eagle's.

When you walk through the valley of the shadow of death, I will be with you.

I will keep you from falling until you joyfully stand blameless in My presence.

Even if your mother forgets you, I will never forget you.

If I look after the sparrows, I will certainly take care of you.

If you remain still, I will do your fighting for you.

The Secret Behind Wisdom

I will give you My power to destroy spiritual strongholds.

I will meet all your needs so you can overflow with good works.

I will give you My strength and bless you with My peace.

I watch over you and I listen for your prayers.

I know everything about you and am mindful of all your ways.

Draw near to Me and I will cleanse you from an evil conscience.

Delight in Me and I will give you the longings of your heart.

If you love Me with all your heart, I will provide all you need.

I am your rock and your salvation, a fortress that cannot be shaken.

You will have perfect peace if you keep focused on Me.

If you pray to Me in secret, I will reward you openly.

I will guide you to the very end, for I will be your God forever.

Every promise that I make is true, for I do not change My mind.

    As I heard all these promises unveil themselves to me, I wondered how can someone remember and honor them, but in assurance the voice said_ I will not forget My promises because I am a merciful God.

You can hold on the hope that I will not

change what I have promised.

Oh Lord! I exclaimed myself... The complexity of life is a quest many of us try to decode. Is it to attain human ultimate height? Or is it to...

Many are those who have given up! They say we were lied to and in return they search for other gods... And, claim it keeps them tranquil in meditation... Yet, I call that abomination.

In the few of us left ... confusion arises and tries to duplicate a sun wake.

They take what is to their advantage and ignore what, is right for life!

Many are we who acclaim this Man they call Jesus ... Jesus Christ.

The atmosphere became light and peaceful as I began to extol Him.

Glory be to you, Shiloh, Peace bringer.

Star of Jacob, Redeemer, Son of God, Son of the Highest, Son of the Blessed, Holy One, King of Kings, Chief corner stone, Rose of Sharon, Lily of the Valleys, Emmanuel.

Counsellor, Mighty God, My Everlasting Father, my Prince of Peace. Jehovah Jireh, Jehovah Nissi,

Jehovah Shalom, Jehova Shammam, Ancient of Days. Messiah, Sun of Righteousness, Jesus of Nazareth, Jesus Christ my Savior, Son of David, Bridegroom, my Master, my Savior, Lamb of God, Adonai, Father.

Bread of Life, my Deliverer, Author and Finisher, Alpha and Omega, Almighty, El Shaddai, Omnipotent, Lion of the Tribe of Judah, Lord of Lords, El Elyon, El Roi, El Yisrael, Yahweh.

Oh my, If and only if, we reflected on the beatitudes... Abba Father.

As my eulogy for the King of Kings was finishing, I heard the soothing echo of voices elevating in praise_

O Lord my God, when I in awesome wonder,

Consider all the worlds Thy Hands have made;

I see the stars, I hear the rolling thunder,

The Power throughout the universe displayed.

Then sings my soul, My Savior God, to Thee,

How great Thou art, How great Thou art.

Then sings my soul, My Savior God, to Thee,

How great Thou art, How great Thou art.

When through the woods, and forest glades I wander,

And hear the birds sing sweetly in the trees.

When I look down, from lofty mountain grandeur,

And hear the brook, and feel the gentle breeze.

Then sings my soul, My Savior God, to Thee,

How great Thou art, How great Thou art.

And when I think, that God His Son not sparing;

Sent Him to die, I scarce can take it in;

That on a Cross, my burden gladly bearing,

He bled and died to take away my sin.

Then sings my soul, My Savior God, to Thee,

How great Thou art, How great Thou art.

When Christ shall come, with shout of acclamation,

And take me home, what joy shall fill my heart.

Then I shall bow, in humble adoration,

And then proclaim; "My God, how great Thou art!"

Then sings my soul, My Savior God, to Thee,

How great Thou art, How great Thou art.

The time came. The time was here. It was time indeed. I walked, ate, slept and heard Him. I now realized that what I did was right.

The journey ahead of me seemed long. It had ups and downs, but was not intimidating. I knew my pillar was one no one could fully describe.

Some things change, and some don't change. It was then and now is now ... I knew that this person some call Melchizedek was fully accessible.

Everything that was said and everything that I heard, was a reality, but who was Melchizedek?

Every question I asked myself, the answer came to me ... and again I asked, who is this Melchizedek?

The Secret Behind Wisdom

This Melchizedek was king of Salem and priest of God Most High. He met Abraham returning from the defeat of the kings and blessed him, and Abraham gave him a tenth of everything.

First, the name Melchizedek means "King of Righteousness", then also, "King of Salem" means "King of peace."

Without father or mother, without genealogy, without beginning of days or end of life, resembling the Son of God, he remains a priest forever.

Just think how great he was: Even the patriarch Abraham gave him a tenth of the plunder! Now the law requires the descendants of Levi who become priests to collect a tenth from the people – that is, from their fellow Israelites – even though they also are descended from Abraham.

This man, however did not trace his descent from Levi, yet he collected a tenth form Abraham and blessed him who had the promises. And without doubt the lesser is blessed by the greater. In the one case, but in the other case, by him who is declared to be living.

One might even say that Levi, who collects the tenth, paid the tenth through Abraham, because when Melchizedek met Abraham, Levi was still in the body of his ancestor.

A smooth breeze went by ... I paused and continued to be enlightened_ If perfection could have been attained through the Levitical priesthood – why was there still need for another priest to come, one in the order of Melchizedek, not in the order of Aaron? For when the priesthood is changed, the law must be changed also. He of whom these things are said belonged to a different tribe, and no one from that tribe has ever served at the altar.

The Secret Behind Wisdom

For it is clear that our Lord descended form Judah, and in regard to that tribe Moses said nothing about priests. And what we have said is even more clear if another priest like Melchizedek appears, one who has become a priest not on the basis of a regulation as to his ancestry but on the basis of the power of an indestructible life. For it is declared:
You are a priest forever, in the order of Melchizedek.

The former regulation is set aside because it was weak and useless (for the law made nothing perfect), and a better hope is introduced, by which we draw near to God.

And it was not without an oath! Others became priests without any oath, but he became a priest with an oath when God said to him:

The Lord has sworn and will not change his mind: You are a priest forever.

Because of this oath, Jesus has become the guarantor of a better covenant.

Now there have been many of those priests, since death prevented them from continuing in office, but because Jesus lives forever, he has a permanent priesthood. Therefore he is able to save completely those who come to God through him, because he always lives to intercede for them.

Such a high priest truly meets our need – one who is holy, blameless, pure, set apart form sinners, exalted above the heavens. Unlike the other high priests, he does not need to offer sacrifices day after day, first for his own sins, and then for the sins of the people.

He sacrificed for their sins once for all when he offered himself. For the law appoints as high priests men in all their weakness, but the oath, which came after the law, appointed the Son, who has been made perfect forever.

Because he always lives to intercede for them … One who is holy, blameless, pure, set apart from sinners, exalted above the heavens. So deep and so true.

Abba father._ The end"

"Impressive Lloyd whispered. That is impressive, I have read the beatitudes over and over in the Bible but never looked at it the way you just read"

"Lloyd" Tiffany mentioned as she stood, "I think I am getting really pulled by the mystery in the Bible, looks like we might take a venture together. I will take some time off after the busy season and study the Bible so I can understand and have all the secrets in it unveiled!"

"You are tapping into the wisdom, knowledge and anointing my friend. I will begin to write the book. I am ready."

"Good call Lloyd. Let's call it a day for now and get back at it tomorrow."

The Secret Behind Wisdom

REFERENCES

Cover design by Blaise Tshibwabwa for Malachi Publications

All poems by Blaise Tshibwabwa for Malachi Publications

Scripture references taken from the Holy Bible – KJV, NIV and AMP versions

Leadership principles from Handbook to Leadership: Leadership in the Image of God by Kenneth B.

Faith and wisdom articles by William B.

The Beatitudes from the book of Mathew in the Holy Bible

Topic on faith from the book of Hebrews in the Holy Bible

Promises taken from the Holy Bible

The complexity of life – Poem by Blaise Tshibwabwa

How great Thou art – Christian hymn composed by Carl Gustav Boberg

Melchizedek from the book of Hebrews in the Holy Bible

The Secret Behind Wisdom

www.ingramcontent.com/pod-product-compliance
Lightning Source LLC
Chambersburg PA
CBHW070547050426
42450CB00011B/2758